All I Need Is A Pen

All I Need Is A Pen

(Poetic Visions)

By: Leonna Brabham

iUniverse, Inc.
New York   Bloomington

Copyright © 2009 by Leonna Brabham

All rights reserved. No part of this book may be used or reproduced by any means, graphic, electronic, or mechanical, including photocopying, recording, taping or by any information storage retrieval system without the written permission of the publisher except in the case of brief quotations embodied in critical articles and reviews.

iUniverse books may be ordered through booksellers or by contacting:

iUniverse
1663 Liberty Drive
Bloomington, IN 47403
www.iuniverse.com
1-800-Authors (1-800-288-4677)

Because of the dynamic nature of the Internet, any Web addresses or links contained in this book may have changed since publication and may no longer be valid. The views expressed in this work are solely those of the author and do not necessarily reflect the views of the publisher, and the publisher hereby disclaims any responsibility for them.

ISBN: 978-1-4401-6385-2 (sc)
ISBN: 978-1-4401-6386-9 (ebook)

Printed in the United States of America

iUniverse rev. date: 11/17/2009

Dedication

To my lord and savior, I am very appreciative for this accomplishment. This book means everything to me. The creation turned out to be terrific. I wouldn't have gotten this far without you and the people you've put in my life. With your guidance I was able to get through this persistently. We made it possible! Your worthiness is indescribable. Though I know there are more goals ahead you've given me faith and wisdom. My spirit is filled with your blessings. I will continue to give you thanks everyday.

For you, my four brothers
Leon, Arnold, Andre and Allen
&
For you, my sister
Ebony and my delighted niece Jaydah

I love you all so much and the feeling is extraordinary!!!!! I can't breathe normally if one of you isn't around. Finally, the talent I've embodied for so long and often spoke about can be shown on paper. When I wrote this book, I thought of you all. To my niece Jaydah, you are bright and progressing very well. You are my little helper. I know you're happy for your auntie. Be good girl! "I'm always watching." Isn't it inspiring and fantastic to have an author representing our family? Your faces give me a reason to make my life meaningful. I couldn't ask God for a better family. I believe your dreams are also flourishing. I thank ya'll for backing me and showing me the most love.

For you, Mom & Dad

I constantly try to be sure the decisions I make in life, will leave the both of you very proud. Your presence means the world to me. I love you both dearly with every breath I take. Bringing me into this world was the right choice. You've raised me well, because of the values and sense of togetherness you've taught my siblings and I, we're tighter than a knot. Mom, you speak highly of me and because of that I want to do more. Dad, you always give me good advice, I am forever your baby girl! Thank you for being loving parents. The best is yet to come! I know the both of you will be very proud as you read on…

Acknowledgements

To both of my Grandmothers (Stephanie and Helen), I love you both unconditionally. You're both great writers. I definitely know where I inherited the talent of writing. A devoted and thoughtful family is the most precious gift I could ever have. Our family is amazing; when we're all together everyone is jovial and grateful. I continuously pray that we all remain healthy and good role models for the following generations. I pray for us to always be there for one another. Also, to build on more prosperity! May God bless you both and may every tear be full of happiness. I thank you both for the help and encouragement.

To my man Teon Blake, you got it going on Babe and that's why I love you! I must acknowledge your support and indulgence in my life. You've helped me become more of a woman. We work well together and I appreciate the attention and affection you've shown me. You always tell me the right things to make me feel good inside and out. You're very smart indeed, you're a good man and you have wonderful parents. Our relationship shall continue to spark with every moment we share. Also, I hope your plans for a brighter future lead to success. I am here for you and thank you for being there for me.

To Ms. Dorothy Ham Arthur of "I Asked and He

Answered," thank you for assisting me with my book through this whole process and giving me good advice. Our God is a great God and I continue to look his way for guidance. Good luck with your books!

Hi! Uncle Norman, I didn't forget you. You are my favorite, I admire your personality. You're full of enthusiasm and it's always a pleasure to have you around. I will never forget the time you read my poems and felt the need to cry; from that day on...... I knew I had a purpose. Thank you for loving my poems, thank you for being humorous and also caring. Last, thank you for always laughing at my jokes.

Kim Gill and Juliann Marchand, I can't explain how grateful I am. I owe both of you big time for taking time out your busy schedules to read over my manuscript; you've helped me out a lot and provided me with editorial suggestions and corrections. I am happy to have met you both during the finishing of my book. There couldn't have been a better time. Thank you for everything and I wish you both well!

All I Need Is A Pen

Let's Begin!

Table of Contents

I.

A Meaningful Approach

Writing has no limits. It is explanatory and expressive. [Experiences jotted] emotions and thoughts. Like creativity, we structure this art using whatever comes to our minds. Still, writing is more than ink and paper; it is a feeling of life and nature. We love it and we live it. For me it has been a given. All I Need Is A Pen and everything will be written.

Leonna Brabham

Art is in the Heart

Draw a heart
What do you see? Art!
The beauty is in you!
What we do-
Resembles,
The skills we have
Controls the path
Of our destiny,
It's in our memory
To fulfill our dreams
In which we believe can prosper
The love,
The faith,
The strive,
The struggle,
And the success of talents
Are so beautiful as we imagine
Despite the devils advocate
In action
We continue to make things
Happen
With all the sports---
And entertainment,
And education,
And careers,
And technology
We keep obtaining
Shows…
Art in the Heart
Like a-
Picture Painting!

Forever Glad

Failure is despair
disappointment we fear
won't break us
down
so we keep around hopes
and dreams
even if the possibility seems-
unpromising,
we continue to think BIG!
and grow strong,
even if time prolongs
we don't setback,
fall, give up
and lack,
we don't fear struggles,
we dare to let discouraging trouble us,
we are a bunch of men and women
coming from tough times of living,
giving is something-
we hardly ever had
so today we're-
Forever Glad!

Wake Up!

Wake up! Wake up! Wake up!
We are the people of color
Why has shame come upon us?
We're brilliant and beautiful like the sky,
We fail to realize and let each other die.
Wake up everybody let's keep dreams alive.
I'll tell you, we ought to be thankful and praising one
another
Look at your mother and father with glory
Despite sad stories
We must continue to live on...

Don't feel sorry for a painful world
Let's make it better for the next boys and girls.
Wake up everybody let's keep dreams alive.
The new generation will soon arrive
Raise them well
They shall prevail
Rich and famous-
Too many of us are still living poor and still struggling-
We deserve more,
Wake up everybody let's keep dreams alive.
We must show one another how to provide
If we do our children will know how to survive!

Negative Contact

We were destructive people that weren't nice
Accompanied by things illegal that wasn't right,
Collectively, my team lied
"Negative contact" we would say…
Our parents were always surprised by our bogus portray.
We stayed fly, pretty and neat
Arriving to school on time
But when our phones beeped
We rolled out like a drop of a dime-
To meet up at once,
If we got the code of drill-
Definitely, we were needed in a rush
To play hooky and cut-
We chilled, got fired up and hung with the guys
Perceiving fashionable and seductive
For them to pay our tides,
Personating the passion of greed
Wasting days and months doing nothing,
Not knowing soon, we would need valuable things-
Worth something, still,
The fights we laid down were awesome,
Troubling other kids instigating problems,
We carried extremely loud
Screaming and cursing
Initiating the crowd
Like a crazed person,
We were a gang
Influenced by negative contact
Now things have changed
Since we moved out the projects

Ambitious

How can I try?
To strive, high
When I am aiming to-
The sky
My hopes are shedding. Why?
Is it me? Or society failing
My ambition is to keep prevailing...
But when a drought comes about
There is a doubt that I won't succeed and
Accomplish what I need.
As time passes by
I continue to try
To think Big and
Dream Large
No one will stop me if I take-
Charge!

Intense Beauty

The shapes we dream to have
Of models (laugh)
Our faces, like the moon, suddenly changes
When we make up our nose, lips and eyes
For a new look and perfect size,
Our naturalness is then disguised.
We whimper over our pillow
And CRY,
And CRY,
And CRY…
Why?
Intense Beauty

Lost

Lost in this world
We call home, choosing to do-
Nothing
But roam. With many things to do, time
Flies by, still no clue,
Lost, trying to find some-
Where to go in a world extremely
Big…We just don't know
Until we learn who we are
And what is meant. And some, well-
They may never-
Ever, get it!!!!!

We Can Be Better

Now we folks know better than that. Steady,
We don't stop the way we act
Walking around confused and unaware
Buying these excuses when opportunities are there
Doing everything except for us
Because society flushes our minds with material stuff
We folks know better than that
Turning our backs when we need each other
Why is it we can't stick together?
Do we blame history for our actions today?
Why do some of us continue to behave this way?
Shattering one another
Meanwhile-
The police keep harassing our brothers

We folks know better than that
Cops want our asses locked and lacked
So we're snatched easy off the streets
To have no freedom or no peace,
This is how families are broken
and left with little token
HOPING…

Let's stop trying to be equal
And become our own people
I believe we can be better-
If we just stick together

First Black President

2008 was the greatest debate
John McCain for the same
Barack Obama for change
We watched and we listened
Those two men
Aim to win-
And then, it happened
In 2009, on November 4th, he was elected
Our First Black President!

Brooklyn

Brooklyn, we not going to give in
This is our borough our house our family land
How dare they try to take over our surface man?
Money can't buy the love we share
It holds much more weight. Brooklyn
We're worth more than what we rate
We came a long... long way
Today is a new day. Patiently,
We wait for plots to settle
Mentally stuck on disorderly conduct
Trying to overcome being a menace to society
Gets hard when communities aren't showing any unity
Seems like they're helping everyone but you and me-

I want to make my space a better place
Is it true I can't crop because of my race?
Black and beautiful, strong and stout, Brooklyn
Do you see what I'm talking about?
A seed that blossoms can face a lot of problems
Confront and resolve them
Can fate determine accomplishment?
I can't see us developing without involvement.

We as a group need to get focalized
Before its too late where we can no longer socialize
Realize goodness appears when you arrive
Creating abnormal statistics
Consciously our mind is realistic
I'm too deep for this. Do you get it?

Brooklyn, we not going to give in
This is the life we live from the beginning to the end
After life is not this, make the best out of this,
Reminiscence the day, first existed
Combined to the mind of someone grown
Missions are now on your own
The people you meet and see might not be the people you think.
Many places to go, different things to know
Get familiar with your worth and determine your monetary wealth
Profit and stabilization
Establish an organization
Understand what I am saying?
I'm relating to anyone paying taxes and rent
We're experiencing a recession. Brooklyn is drastically changing-
We need to get down with it

The Test

In the mind of a man
Who knew one day he would land
In a place he could not stand and bear to dare to climb
He closed his eyes and became blind
To what we call choice and chance of one's own mind
Following behind a ghost designed as human flesh.
It was evilness he had to escape-
Trapped walls with sharp ceilings he would soon face
From drugs and alcohol
He been through it all
Instead of choosing the right path of guiding light
He slept alone in a dark room day and night
He was doomed.

Traced with thoughts of wickedness
On his conscious-
He twisted and turned side to side
Leaving his self breathless,
He shivered back and forth
Suddenly a chill, goose bumps and cough,
He became numb.
Realizing he was dumb the whole time
To not see the ghost designed as human flesh
He looks in the mirror (stunned)
And began to guess
Finally his eyes are wide open
Still, he fails the Test
Wake Up Before It Is You Put To Rest!

Where Is The Justice?

Justifications should be giving no hesitations
Cops continue to get away with false accusations
Leaving the victimized no explanations
Where is the civilization to prosecute the abomination?
There should be no toleration in this nation.

A crime should not be justified when a man is shot
numerous times-
With no cruel intensions on his mind
Why is law then turned around and being legitimized?
In their eyes he was a menace to society, No!
We are the endangered species.

They have the right to kill no matter how victims feel
Accurate justifications are not being revealed. So,
More and more innocent people are being killed
That's not fair. But,
Is it fair for criminal thugs to shoot their peers?

It is not and cops are there for them to stop
Simmering on what they plot,
Don't excuse my righteousness
Where is the justice? For all the killings and slaughters that
did it.
Come forth with information? Stop! With the
discrimination

We need more black people in corporations
Not being races, its basics.
Look at these unfamiliar faces
Can't help us out of misery by killing our families
You did it, admit it
Pulling the trigger before he was admitted, I'm not with it

We lacking republic
Where is the justice?

Temptation of the Bees

Circling ones possession

Heading the wrong

Direction, soon you'll

Learn your lesson.

Magnetically attracted

Mentally distracted,

Temptation of the bees

Harassing,

Following negativity

Sidetracking capability,

Don't let temptation catch you

Running from potential

We are the People

We are the people
We are the voice
We are the body
We are the mind

Let us combine one prime into this nation
Stop wasting time
The government is not in our favor
It has been designed for us to lack on paper
Get on your feet
Become a part of this set
Create more power and unity
Help us bring more money to-
Prosper our communities.
We are the people
We are the voice
We are the body
We are the mind

To protect,
Follow in our steps, to
Process a net-
We can respect
Listen to these words of wisdom
Envision the goal to control
This land for once!
We are the people
We are the voice
We are the body
We are the mind

No longer behind.
We are the history of today
Let us not be slaved and betrayed no way
We are worth more than minimum wage
We are the people of this modernize world
Young boys and girls get up!
Take each other's hand
Take a stand and let us hear your plans
Speak up! Come forth with your thoughts
Do not keep them hidden
They see us rising and striving
And know what rebellion means
Do not believe your dreams are forbidden
Look we have driven them away…
Wake up everybody today is the day!
No more stealing our knowledge
When colleges accept us
They think we're all in jail, well-
There are still enough of us
We can get a higher education without a fuss
For once our president is black!
So times have changed remember that…
We are the people
We are the voice
We are the body
We are the mind

In office at this time!

Who Would've Thought?

You thought I was stupid until I said "Sophisticated"
Now you look at me wise and authentic
You thought I was ugly until I showed my true colors
Now I'm looking good amongst others
You thought I was sassy until I put on a gown
Now you are the one trying to be down
You thought I was ghetto until I moved out the hood
Now you are the one doing no good
You thought I didn't have any manners until I said "My Grace"
Now you are looking shocked in the face
You thought I couldn't get the job until they said "I was hired"
Now you are the one who is fired
You thought I would fail until I prevailed
Now you are the one not doing so well
You thought I was wrong until I made the right choice
Now you watch me, as I rejoice
You thought I would never be happy until I stop being sad
Now you are the one extremely mad
You thought I wouldn't love again until I found a new friend
Now you are the one trying to come back in
You thought I wouldn't make it
But Who Would've Thought?

Homeless Mess

Living outside in raggedy, smelly clothes

Pushing shopping carts, with cans to recycle,

Beat up sneakers and shoes

Walking around looking a disgrace

Asking people for change

All in their face,

Sleeping on the train

Digging in the garbage

Searching for food

Because they're starving,

Craving for something to eat

In need of shelter and

A better atmosphere to sleep

Homeless mess

Judge them not less

Everyone has a story

To protest!

Time to Make a Change

To the readers, viewers and listeners who had enough
Put down that cup of alcohol
Put down that blunt
Put down that gun
And listen up!
We need to socialize
Come together and utilize

Time to make a change

Look at your surroundings, Brooklyn will no longer be the
same
While construction is being place
Do not be a destruction laying waste
Get involved; stop acting bored
Everything will come as accord.
We need money to build also,
A Great Mind to prevail
A wise idea is good enough
Keep in mind "Never Give Up"
Some people want the minority to stop, drop, fail and bail
Do not give them the benefit we can be swell
Fascinated like children's fairytales'
Go ahead be thorough, ask for a piece of your borough.

The time is now make a change

Family and friends will be amazed to see unity
Hit that stage,
Establishing with collaboration

Where do you want to live?
Tomorrow is not promise
What about your kids?
Get a job, work hard, go to school follow the rules
We can still be cool
Libraries have plenty resources for us to learn
Come on... let's go be that warm
If you have talent do not quit
Soon someone will notice it
Schedule yourself
Need some help?
Ask around, someone is waiting
For you to "Browse"
Trust me you will be proud
Do not be afraid to be brave
There is always a person who wants to be saved!

Glass of Water or Wine Please

Working all day
and cooking
and cleaning
I deserve a break-
taking care of my kid's
and man too...
with little help from you-
I'm tired,
my body is aching
I need a vacation.

Four hours of sleep
then back up again
washing, ironing and driving
I was sexing all....... night
I'm tired
someone give me a glass of water, please!
or wine,
I need a drink of mine!

The Tradition

When we ate dinner at
Grandma's house
It was delicious. Everyone-
favored her tradition,
We gathered together wearing pretty dresses and
nice ties, all to suit-
Grandma's home made pies.
Telling jokes and laughing
hilariously, enjoying family time and
Grandma was always the best-
she cooked every soul food dish to name...
Thanksgiving, Christmas time, New Years, Easter and
Birthdays were all the same,
Folks grew older...
Days started to change
Relatives split to towns in Jersey,
Pennsylvania, Georgia, Upstate, Down South and
Virginia, while others-
Stayed in the city as I remember,
We started a new traveling tradition-
Where everyone cooked a dish and
brought a gift,
Anxious and jolly to see one another
From mother to father-
Sister to brother-
Aunts to uncles-
Cousins to friends and in-laws...
All related no matter what-
we were called
Listening to music, playing cards and games,

catching up, on the good O days,
Stepping to beats and
Singing songs,
This went on and on…
Then it came time to say "good-bye" and
Everyone would drive away-
Until next time

Forbidden

When goodness appears for me
Through strives and remedies...
No one cares to see, how-
That came to be.
Apparently, they feel terrible inside
Though they try to hide

I know, they have nothing
To show and tell, and
Rather than see me prevail
They rather me fail
This would suit them well
Taken the fact they not doing so well

Well, isn't that bad and
Aren't they dumb?
To think I'll be like them
With no agenda, fame
And no clue-
Of what to do

Clocking the art of my style
They began to frown
Can't see me happy so,
They put me down and
Begin to judge me profound
Until my deepest secretes are found.

I say, "You won't devastate my fate"
This is my space and my grace

I'll quickly tell them…
"Get out of my face"
Unless they want to succeed
Willing to learn how to earn
What they need.

Life is not easy, to win it
You have to get it, without quitting
Doing things the hard way
Will leave you FORBIDDEN!!!!
My advice is;
Stop now if you're going the wrong way
Because when it's your time to portray an image
You'll be standing and staring stuck without luck
Wishing you made the (right decision) from the jump!

Retribution Will Come

We need not
to look at our opponents
and fear worry or grief
they're the sheep
let the lion-
represent our roar…
we're the affirmative
when we are called…
let them hear our sound
an instrumental crowd,

Down in the dirt
where we dug for land and gold
we'll bury their souls.
on this journey we plan to take off-
let us not be afraid to come forth
for retribution will come
for each and everyone

Awaken from Wonderland

Growing up
She lived in wonderland
Daydreaming constantly
About where she stands
Until one day she was awaken
By a master plan
Tired of being broke and
Empty-handed, watching TV-
Sitting on the couch stranded
Looking at people nice cars-
Big houses and designer clothes
Saying "one day she would get those"
She couldn't sleep
Until she got off her feet to seek
Applying herself to the streets, and No!
She wasn't selling weed
Dope and crack
For any man
Sure no hoe, scam,
She had a mindset plan-
To be rich and famous
Spending money wisely
Living life painless,
Hoping this feeling could last
Forever, showing more love than
Ever, thanking God for being
Blessed, starting with
Less, ending with the best!
Remembering the days
Where she had nothing

Wishing she could give the whole world
Something, cherishing-
Ever moment of bliss
Smiling back at-
The first time she ever
Pictured this...
Making a big change
Self-determination could explain
She went from no name
To fame
Waiting for you to wake up and
Do the same!

School is Cool

School is cool
That's why we should go
To learn and know more than before,
Getting a higher education is a self-motivation
To be proud and receive consolation means everything-
Like our money and bling-bling
But, the key to success
Is achieving our best, in the process
Leading others along the way can pay.
We must have the knowledge to work toward our dreams
and think (clever) when it comes to unaffordable needs
Big spenders know what I mean
It's the drive to strive that pushes us to succeed!
So go to school
You can still be cool

Teenage Peer Pressure

Tied to a barricade of violence
caught up in the projects
born and raised
in a rage of trouble
young folks stumble.
fallen, into temptation
mistaken, with false accusations
seen with the enemy
on the block- at
the spot, risking to be
knocked, sure enough
before a chance to stop-
the cops had you locked.

You were different. But,
you did not listen
it was your decision
to be in jail
with your crew
pick your friends
do not let them
pick you!

Train Dump

Attention;
I'm on the stage listen
Everyone have to get on the train
Before they miss it
Time machines are fiction
Clocks are ticking
Who's watching me?
Thinking I'm beneficial
Its official

Not bashing me over the head
With your stereotypical mess
I suggest you get lost
Before I am forced to
Make you feel even less
I bet if I had the best diamond necklace
You'll be driven reckless
and a pair of five hundred dollar shoes and
Gucci bags, you'll be mad
But why wish for what I have?

Personally;
If you get on this train here
The ride would not be longer than
You standing there
Want some profit crop it
Procrastinate; be late getting established
Working should be a habit
Like heroin and crack, weed and cigarette packs
Negative contact

I'm riding and riding with this-
Train of thought
How many people want to be like the boss?
Raise your hand with a plan
Stand, all types of people are in this cart
It doesn't matter where you're going
It's how you start
Superior of the way you walk and talk
You are not inferior
You are not a puppet; you are not a hawk
Unless you've been caught

Those that don't move chooses to loose
and lessen their worth
Someone said "I wasn't down to earth" so,
I asked... what does that suppose to mean?
I'm not what it seems
Because I have fantasies
and dreams
Like please, wake up
Everyone can't be prompt
Well, I said, "Until my time is up...
I will not be a junk-
Living on a Train Dump

No More Violence!

Whoever you are
Wherever you from
Put down that gun

Time to stop the violence

No more tolerance
No more fighting's
No more killings

Let's all put an end to the nonsense
Easier said than done
Please put down that gun!
There's more importance in life
We as the people can make it right

Look at your peers
Look at your friends
Look at your parents
Look at your siblings

Let's stop and look at the youth
What is the new generation going to go through?

I want to make a difference like the leaders of the past
What about you? Let's all follow their path
Communities are coming to an end
Some people don't want us here
Should they win?

That's not fair
Do you know anything about democracy?
That's the Government who handles polices
Let's show them we're worth more than their hypothesis

Women and Men
Boys and Girls
Let's come together like families
To get the same affiliation like candidacies
Without violence and more knowledge
Because we're brainy just like those who graduated from
college

The New Us

On the bus we go-
out of Brooklyn Borough
out of New York…
away from the drama
away from fear we thought-
would never disappear,
leaving behind the life of pain and
suffering and struggles
we snuggle together as a couple
never wanting to look back
on the ways we use to act
watching our kids grow to know-
they have a chance with a new life
Preferred
instead of living in urban communities where some dreams
are
Deferred
we look at each other and laugh with happiness and joy
remembering the days we were broke and poor
without a home of our own
now we're grown
living the life we planned-
from the jump
helping people along the way to-
achieve what they want

Exhaustion

Exhausted from sorrow
Hopes for better days tomorrow

Heart-broken instantly
When something troubles us mentally

Trying to resemble righteousness
Steady something ticks our conscience

Linked to the mind
Designated for us to find hope,
Weak and shackled against the rope, we choke

Falling beneath the sky
Lower and lower, then
We began to strive, high

Tired of being a quitter
Unhappy and bitter

Can't give up now after strolling around-
Up's and down's, obstacles

Lend a hand, help out
Leaving us stranded, abandoned in the world single-handed

Dragging along a difficult route, help out
Poor, bored and hungry for food and comfort-
Friends and family torn and broken left with bare token

See us starving and filthy drooling from the mouth
Asking for change, help out,

We've been called naughty, stupid, inadequate and different
Lazy and selfish to blear focus, strangled and feared
hopeless
Depressed and distressed over less portion

Will we ever be all right with this mental fight?
Called life EXHAUSTION

Teacher

Please show me the way
To a brighter day
I want to learn
To earn

TEACHER

I listen to you speak
As you teach
Lessons to the class
I admire the brains you have

TEACHER

You reflect an image of hope
A mentor sincerely devote
Skilled and proficient
To the people who is listening

TEACHER

Show me the way to success
Where I can aim to do my best
Completion of task
Is all I ask? From you-

TEACHER

Suspicious

Curious about your next move
Don't mean to sound rude, but dude
What are your intentions?
For this new dimension
I'm getting a little suspicious
Aware of every aspect
Analyzing the whole concept
You want to take over our projects
Settling in sections
I get the message
Stacking bricks
I want in.

Suspicious

When the job is done
What will be the outcome?
As a result of:
Rebuilding, reconstruction, renovation in our locations
How about some participation
Towards our expectations
Where's the administration?
I want to fill out an application
Take a look at my occupation
With a picture perfect illustration
I would like to be apart of your organization
Along with some of my associations
What do you say?
Can we have some affiliation?
We are skilled and we have bills
We should have the right to work in your field.

Suspicious

Over the years we have tried
I'm curious like George
Why have we been denied?
Seriously, what do you have plan for me?
Intentions of slavery
Those days are history
I won't think of it as that
Unless someone reacts
Try to send us colored folks back-
To the South picking cotton
Those times haven't been forgotten
Go ahead continue to crop…
Finish the plot
I'll stand over here
Don't come near
Otherwise people will call me Ms. Coretta Scott
I'm not lying
I'll be Rosa Parks, tired
Matter of fact they'll call me who I am
I'll make a difference I know I can
A new model
Ringing bells for this generation
I'm not tolerating immoral interrogation
No more cross-examination
Like; are you Hispanic, Asian, Black or White?
Why should it matter?
When we are all human
Isn't that right

I'm suspicious!

Intervention as to Intervene

This dimensional world is conveying our space
Sending messages-
Signs designated for us to trace,
Which way should we go?
Our mindset is-
We already know. Right from wrong
Something urges us to not go on-
So we prolong.

Sidetracking our main aspect
Of life-
Steady longing.............for success
Why is it we choose to go a different route?
Interfering with things we really care about
Again something intervened
Led us to believe tomorrow we'll
Redeem.

We wanted prosperity
Instead negativity was brought around-
And everything we ever wanted started to
Fall down.
That's when our sense of mind
Said;

Stop! Bashing our heads
Clowning us continuously
Knifing our brains
Driving us insane

Consciously we can't retain
Medication pulls us from the pain
Stop! The Intervention
Time to make a change

Unseen Power

In a zone
We live alone
As residence
Abandoning our intelligence
Killing our brain cells
Over and over again we fall apart
Because we don't know how and where to be smart
We fail each other.
From mother to father
We see no possibility to strive
Why?
Because when we were young there were no pushes and
concerns
Whether we learned or not,
Our parents were too busy drinking and smoking pot,
Now we're grown
On our own
Striving to be different and wise
For the sake of our children lives

He Left

He left-
Off, to military land
We watched him go,
To grow, into a stronger man
It happened all too fast,
Before we knew it
He was home at last.
Then off he went back-
To serve his country
In Iraq,
We prayed for his return-
Safe and alive,
Years and months went by-
Still, no reply
We didn't know if he would show.
No letters were mailed
Nor were we phoned.
Afraid, afraid of him,
Not coming home
We wondered the day he left
If he'll be back again,
Then it was him
Announced over the radio,
Brave and honor
Was what we heard
In everybody words
We waited and waited
Anxiously and excitedly
For our hero to return

From A Brother In Jail Perspective

Read between the lines-
People have taken our (lives away),
Thrown us in jail like animals locked in cells
Swept off the streets for them to build in peace
See, ya'll folks don't get it
This is one big (gimmick)
I will admit…We've given them reason without a doubt
But, not everything they've talked about
Was true, still-
They rather believe you then I
Because the way our government has been designed.
All this time for a nickel and dime hustler
When there're people worst killing each other
So, why the federal law investigated us?
Where was the big bust?
It was all about the money
I'm not anybodies' (dummy)
I watched closely and listened,
The way they grabbed us all at once
Was decisional from the jump
They planned to lock us up.
I could have been a better man
Instead hand cuffs were thrown across my hands
Those lying bitches
Said "they were working with snitches"
Well, where's the evidence?
If I was such a big balla$$$$$$
I would've hired a high paid lawyer
To set me free,
Writing those articles about me
Was false and wrong,
I am not suppose to be doing this long…………..

To Death Do Us Part

He came, strolling my way
Fully clad, like a man in a fairytale book
His look, disguised, dark as night
His teeth glistened like light
My inner-self sparked with every step I watched

Closer and closer he got
I began to smell something, something like a rose

He chose to keep me breathing
An oath he planed to treasure
How could he love me dusted like powder?
Me, crypt beneath, enclosed by pleasure
I could only see a dead flower

Slowly he approached me, softly, like fallen petals
I began to smell something, something like a rose

I arose from silence in his conscious
He felt me coming back, such nonsense to think that
I was buried with every memory he hoped
Still, he visited me though I never spoke
To give me a gift he promised if, I should ever go...

With love and zeal
I began to feel something, something like a rose

I reached out, but, my eyes remained closed
I couldn't see, I only pictured what it would be like to touch
His familiar face, I wanted so much to hold

But I could only receive a stem from him
That will soon also die alone

I dreamt….. I was alive and real
But, I could only feel something, something like a rose-

Fall down my grave, he froze
I captured his heart
All I could remember was "to death do us part"
Through my coffin, I could never, ever, impose his offerings
So there I lay with something, something I think is a rose

Innocent Birth

Born into a world full of differences
I was innocent
I began to see no humanizing
People fighting people without socializing
No matter what color and what race the place-
The face and the shape discriminate around the world.
Everything encountered materialism,
Love faded the Universe and hatred was created amongst us
Regulations settled in plantations
Breaking up homes and family relations-
From time to time we suffer from this crime in our nations.
Experiencing favoritism, racism and criticism
Defined as judgmental
I was innocent.
Not wanting to indulge in life negativities was hard for me
With persuasive difficulties
I became accustomed to immoralities
Not familiarize with responsibilities
Steady living in commodity communities,
Before long, I began to see a life not for me
Trying so hard to stop the wickedness
Steady shamefulness came to us
Dreaming to be famous
I was innocent and blameless.
So, I woke up and said "let's be enthusiastically smart"
Start to be apart of what our ancestors cropped
Optimistically sharp!!!!!!
Finally, the disobedience had to stop
Working from the bottom to the top
Being a failure I will not.

Saved by my thoughtful ways
Good-bye to the awful days
I'm innocent
Intentions are to behave
Generosity is where to aim
No more animosity to hypotheses
My policy is now less hatred
Whoever was your enemy, is now your favored
No longer are we material beings and consumers
Nor losers working for minimum wage an hour
We have devoured those days to secure power.
Well, maybe back then you could call me sin
But, I am still innocent
And you, become who you are star!
The direction is not far
There are no more excuses for lacking
We live in a new era what happen?
You slacking get up off your ASS, stop acting
Blaming people for your own actions,
My kids and your kids and their kids
Not going to live like we did,
Having fun and being dumb
Let's start teaching them........when they're young
From day one-
Born our parents angel
That's why they named you
Innocent!

Finally, He found His self

Running from perfection
Heading the wrong direction
Taking mistakes as a lesson
He found his self in a session, alone
Consciously alone,
Mentally stuck in a zone
Unaware of the consequences he will face
With the risks he continues to take…

Burdens of pressure
Hits him like hurricane weather

Distressingly obsessed with possessions from his past
He uses this as an excuse for what he doesn't have
Back and forth, at it again
With this evil self he calls his "friend"
He has to guess what appears to be next
Unless he'll be nothing but stressed,
Outdoors seems less than what he's destined
He must account for more,
Realizing what he has in store
Finally, he found his self knocking at the door
Entering a world where most people are destructive
Can't be apart of that,
He chooses to be more constructive-
Like; becoming about of something, stopping at no course
Now, he is no longer lost

Not For Me

Determined to be a winner I continue to flow like a stream in the river
Walking the earth surface as a person aiming purpose
No longer am I a puppet with strings attached-
Controlled by people and places, and things that held me back,
See, living life in poverty-Not for me
Getting well-fare checks and food stamps-Not for me
Living in low income projects-Not for me
Riding on the bus and train-Not for me
Making minimum wage-Not for me
Screaming and cursing and fighting-Not for me
Felonies and misdemeanors and convictions and evictions-Not for me
Lost time and crime-Not for me
In debt-Not for me
Upset-Not for me
I will succeed and I will get out, that's what I'm about
No time to lack because my parents are black
I'll be the breadwinner. Big spender-
Support families and friends with shelter and dinner.
Time to get saved and behave-
We are not dumb; God gives us strength and wisdom to be strong between right and wrong
Born into sin we were then, now we have grown to own...
We've been hurt and abused and used by those same people that were confused
Here's your chance to prove to be better or bitter
Whether past events still exist there's ways to get over it
Misery-Not for me

I've been blessed
I'm not possessed and stressed and depressed and sick
anymore
From door to door learning and determined to be a winner
I continue to flow like a stream in the river
Walking the earth surface as a person aiming purpose!

Lost Without a Trail

If you every lost a son, daughter, mother, father-
Sister, brother, friend or pet
It was not the end I bet,
I know it hurts painfully, memories of the past
Especially the connection ya'll had,
Can't stop the tears from fallen
You want to see them again,
I know you miss them down on earth
Every birth is not meant to work, why?
Scientifically we don't exam a physical world by only land
We are natural by hand,
Lost souls are taking where? Have you gone there?
To a place we don't trace
Bodies erase off the earth surface
Can heaven be security safe?
Can hell be escaped?
Population increases by woman having babies. Fact,
Is that more punishment to contact?
Can't relax, woman bleed and climax
Pregnant for nine months, children are genetically touched
Magically angels, here to make things better
But, with the chances of weather changing and problem
facing-
It is difficult to prosper,
The devil is a liar.
Where there is love there is hate
Where there is good there is bad
Where there is happy there is sad
Where there is a positive there is a negative
Where there is found there is lost

Where there is hope there is despair
Where there is courage there is fear
And where there is birth there is death
Why do we go through such mess?
Increases and decreases, does that make sense?
Logically believe in faith
There is a better place.
Animals are living things too. See,
They suffer just like you and me produced and brought into
existence
We need to be persistent and have patience
Be strong for tomorrow and let our capabilities follow
Fight responsibility, work to better our communities.
Lost ones maybe watching because their spirits are not
forgotten
Another question: will we reunite someday?
That's an answer neither could portray,
Pray for a better place and a better way
You can run but you can't hide,
The eyes are always watching you and I,
Signs are designated for us to follow pointed towards today
and tomorrow
Where? I don't know until I go
Two paths: the dark alley and guiding light
Wrong or right,
Looks the same but it's a confidential ball game
Individually sustained
Consciously retained,
Which one would you choose? Listen
There are facts written on paper exaggerated,
Confiscated,
Chance is possibility

Risk is consequently,
Don't be scared there is always hope
Humanizing yourself into the pope,
Throughout centuries and decades things appeared
abnormal
Do we continue to fault the past?
I'm ready to establish my future draft
Craft the art of my path,
We live in a dangerous and risky society
Don't be confused by means of reality
Fictionally trapped in a fairytale
In actuality life is not meant to fail
Lost ones gone without a trail

II.

Spiritually Enlightened

When we hear a speech through lecture and any lyrics of measure, our mood suddenly changes. No longer do we respond the same. It is ok- we are embodied to do that. God is our provider he shows us the way; this is why we continue to pray and give him thanks everyday.

Leonna Brabham

Born Again

God, I ask…to
Release these thoughts off my conscious
Give me reason to stop this nonsense. I want out
Praying for these feelings to go away
They don't. At lease not yet-
Steady bashing me, harassing me with hostility and
negativity and animosity
The calamity is a disastrous nightmare worst than death-
With every breath I've taken and ever stepped
There's little strength left
I'm fallen beneath the wind
Feeling my soul weaken
Help me.

God I ask…for
A new path, what listings do you have?
Here I am, take me as I am
Into the sky where a place-
Is better than alive
Born again, without sin
Does after life exist?
Consist of righteousness and bliss
I don't want to give up. But,
I am stuck without luck
I can feel my legs in shock
The impact slowly nabbing at my heart, Stop!

Driven away for a moment, silence
Thought I was done
Steady choking

Stuffing my face with calories too … fat in the first place
Look at me a waste
Even asleep my dreams are deep
Like the ocean and sea drowning beneath this earth
The birth of me was the enemy.
Her water broke
There I was crying, bloody and naked
Can I be born again?
Resurrected

I Made It

From down in the dirt
Where roots grow
I made it
To the sky where birds fly
I made it
Though traffic tried to stop me from going about
I succeeded another route
I made it
I made it
I made it!!!!!!!!!!!!

On The Right Path

We woke up this morning tired
Distressed about the day to come
Can't be hired
Broke again
I got's to be dumb
Unfortunate, unsuccessful unlike that one
Look at her and him
Happy and adequately satisfied
Tired of trying to pretend
Hounding to be recognized
Journeying down the road
Where the sky is gray
And the jewels are not real gold
We continue to pray
For a better class
Prospering persistently
On the right path!

The Love of Life

Love, don't hate each other
appreciate one another
for life's existence
are not our decisions
we're all terrific!
some people don't get it
we are designed
to deliberate from the mind
into the world we adapt
judged on how we act
giving opportunities to perform duties
see, life is full of prosperity
influenced by a lot of negativity
differences, resemblances and experiences
throughout nations expectations
we're taught from old generations
A life born the same
until we change
manifested out the nest
growing like a seed
developing into human beings
visualized individually
as we see:
whoever we are
whatever we know
whenever we show
wherever we go
A shadow is found somewhere around
to lead us till dust
A secret to life

is the attraction of what we like!
follow your own dreams and pray for honor
for every hour and every minute and every second
people are dying
people are crying
never give up trying
show the world you can be pro
before it is your time to go
enjoy life now
while you are still around
believe it or not
life customs don't ever stop!

God Is Worthy

I was told God was first
Then he created the heavens and the earth
He made animals and man
All by hand

As time started to change
The world no longer was the same
People erupted with power
And began to devour

Symptoms of human begins took place
There was a battle of God's grace
More and more evil things appeared
As darkness smeared

God's flourishing creation came and went
As more and more people began to sin
A place of Paradise was no longer bliss
Because God did not grant crisis

There was always a choice of decision-making
Before an urge was mistaken
Whether to do right or wrong
As one continued on

But just like now some people don't know how
To be carefully profound
Instead they choose to be fed
The worst way said...

God is incredibly worthy out of sight
As to light he is might
Believe in his doings of day one
For he is said to be, the man that gave his only begotten son

Rollercoaster Ride

Take me high,
High up to the sky
Rollercoaster ride,
Get me there fast-
Fast as you can
My seat belt is buckled
I am ready to meet him.
Rollercoaster ride
Fly, fly, and fly
Sunlight is waiting for me to arrive,
In amusement
I can hear the music
A jubilee's celebration
In dedication, for my passage to heaven
I am sweating
I am screaming
I am anxious,
A new world is ready to greet me as their acquaintance
Rollercoaster ride scurry
I am in a hurry
My journey is near by-
Please! Let me off this rollercoaster ride.

Along The Way

Trust in the way
Along judgment day
O' lord save me now
Before my spirit is found
Follow me through
Faith onto you
I believeth in thou name
In God we Trust
Thou fame,
Shall I not dishonor thee
For the light I will see
Free from this earth
Of sinful birth
Thou showiest the way
Along judgment day

Judgment Day

We say life ends then begins again
Only then will we ever know when
Judgment day waits
Specifically, who knows the exact date?
To everyone God is coming back
As the world would be attached

The man who created this art
Will determine our departure
From righteously and sinning in the heart
Well, I'll tell you…
Life for me hasn't been so blue
There's all types of (shit) I been through
But yet, I have not heathen to hell
I've said my grace to prevail…

So, I'll swell my way to his place
On judgment day,
Leaving behind those people in disbelief
Pleading, as they lay bleeding beneath
I shall save my soul
For God heavenly mole
Before I burn to flesh and nothing is left

For, God is my Shepard and I shall be protected
On judgment day, to not be rejected
We must pray and believe
What we are facing is real
We must stop the bitterness and disgracing now
Before it's too late and we don't know how

Our Lord path is a swift draft
He'll come just that fast
For us,
As he considers his love and trust
To dust
For us
On judgment day

She Got Saved

It was depressing the way she behaved
She said… she wouldn't do it no more
But turned around and did the same thing as before
Nobody thought she would ever change
Until that day came and she got saved!

Hire Me Please

So, do I get the job? We will call you
That's exactly what I was afraid of-
No love
I come dressed in office attire, showing my sophistication
Not satisfyingly enough
(Impossible)
That does not motivate me
On a job hunt to retrieve maybe

HIRE ME PLEASE

Am I eligible? Qualified for the position?
What are the requirements needed?
Do I not fit the description?
I am professionalized
Sit there and judge me equalized
I am focalized
Look at my resume I am standardized

HIRE ME PLEASE

I am confident you will be pleased
And thrilled to have me on your team
What do you mean I am not supreme?
I've just shown you my recommendations
Still don't believe
Here's my best performance
I'm not acting, this is important

HIRE ME PLEASE

I am not begging, I am intellectual and skilled
Let it be shown what I can do is educationally fundamental
Morally developed easily
A job is what I need to gross increasingly
You need me
I am potentially and equally ready

HIRE ME PLEASE

A Thankful Prayer

Now it's time for bed
Prayers are said…
Thanks for mommy and thanks for daddy
Thank you for my siblings-
Family and friends
Thank you for being there for me
When no one else could see
Thank you for keeping my spirit optimistic
So that I won't quit
Thank you for showing me hope
When no one else spoke
You gave me luck when I wanted to give up
God you are great
You give me faith to live each day
Without you I have no clue
Of what to do
You're the guide to my light
You make sure I am all right at night
I appreciate the people you put in my life
And though, I know
We all must go some day
I can't wait
To finally say…Thanks!

Don't Quit go for It

Fortunate to have lived this life
Good and bad
Wrong and right
I choose this path
Learning from experiences
From presumptuous to prosperous
Given the opportunities
I didn't quit
I went for it
As obstacles came upon
I prayed to God
Not only when times were hard
I always thanked him in regard.

When preventions and provocations came along
I dwelt with con,
Choosing what I thought was best for me
Handling my responsibility
See, I learned life wasn't easy
Don't make it hard
There are:
Jubilant places with bliss
Beautiful faces to miss
Worldly spaces to enrich
With persistence, practice and precaution
I stayed focused
On me
With who and what I wanted to be!

Today is the Day

Today is the day
To just get up and do it,
Forget about everything
And everyone for a minute,
This is your time
To utilize...... your capabilities
There are plenty of opportunities out here
Don't fear,
Whether feeling tension or stress
From only four hours of rest
Today is the day
To throw all excuses away,
Broke or not
God will lead the way
We have to start somewhere and somehow
So the time is now!

Courage From Within

Let this poem enlighten your day
Inspire you to get up and pray
For a better way
Let this poem lead your visions on the right mission
When you make a decision in your life
Today,
Be confident that you will make a difference.
Listen to these words of wisdom
Stop!
For a minute
Imagine a thing you wish to have
Dream a place you want to be
Now say….."Time to do me"
Get up on your feet and seek
What you think
In your mind,
Put aside friends and family
Seeming not, to understand……. what
You have in plan.
Do not be discourage
Have faith in yourself
Believe you can achieve
And you will succeed!
Start in your heart by working from the bottom-
To the top
Do not quit
Do it, NOW
Do not give up, EVER
Only you can make your life better!

Moment

It does count
Who said it don't
Better watch out
Dis' ani't no joke

Instantly, we appeared
Onto the earth
Momentarily we forget who cared
Until things start to hurt

As we grow
Into human beings
We learn to know
Different things

Continuing to only eat the fruit
Like that matters the most
Rotting the root
Until it turns into ghost

Only for a moment
We realize what is done
Then it becomes important
To pray for a better one

Once Known

the time has come
for me to depart
this earth
my remembrance will forever
be in your heart
since birth
I was born
to be what I've become
at this time my mission is done
I'll leave back my dreams and
legacies
to forever be known throughout history
moments shared with you
has been incredible
but now I must go and
bare myself mute
don't worry my place here
will be filled
it's been real and fun
we shall meet again
when judgment day comes…
fear not my being
you are still living here and
you're not alone
so may your days be pleasant
as I once known…

To a Friend in Heaven

Hi friend
I guess you know life after death
Since you left the earth it hurts.
Are you playing hide and seek?
I can't find you anywhere on concrete
I wonder...........when I look up at the sky
Are you passing by?
I miss you friend in sight
We were so tight,
Now your physical nature is no longer fleshed
But your everlasting soul is left
You're an angel watching over me
To do my best!

He Said. . .

The opportunity for living was empty
It seemed imperfect at that moment
I was hurting
I didn't care what people thought or said.......to me,
I was better off dead
No one showed me love and no one cared
I was always left alone in my room to cry in tears
Cracking my knuckles and staring at the ceiling
Listening to songs and raps that related to my feelings
Writing lyrics...
I was haunted by a curse and thinking the worst-
Thoughts in my head
That's when I felt God and he said...
"You are here for many reasons like four seasons"
I didn't understand at first
Until I seen the meaning written in my verse
It wrote: my gift to the earth
At that moment my intensions for leaving was gone
I began breathing different from that day on

High School Diploma

New faces to see and
places to go
how could they not know?
this would be challenging for me
I disliked the rules
so how in hell was I expected to finish high school?

First year I did well
then I began to fail
popularity came
everyone knew my name
security was on my back
deans blamed me for this and that

Then there were the boys
I impressed, flattering them the way I dressed
and the girls who hated my guts
next the cuts
I didn't go to class
so my chances to pass were poor

Teachers expected much more out of me
but I was to busy being lazy and pretty
I couldn't see-
how smart I really was
then, I got a buzz and
saw life for what it was

Settling for a G.E.D
could've been good enough
for me
I hated the work
my teachers sucked
but I never gave up

Now today
I frame my diploma
along with my degree
though it wasn't easy
I knew I had to do it
For me!

Priority First

Staying up late
working all............night
still, I have the strength
to wash and clean
and iron my clothes.
this is how it goes…
I am a woman on time
can't let a day go by without
setting priorities straight
so I am awake,
bright and early
feeling worldly wise
and organized,
showering and gathering things at night
I am sure things will go right in my life
every morning I am up
still a little tired
but, so what
giving thanks to God for the day to come
and the days ahead
he is the main reason I get out of bed.
I've been blessed
there's no need to complain or to get stressed
there're too many people out here with less
and some with more
so the life I live
I continue to adore!

Life For Me Isn't Easy
(From A Man)

Feeling tipsy
off this Hennessey
dizzy and numb
chewing gum
Life for me isn't easy.

Stuck and wasted
kissing my girl
she could taste it,
I was drunk face it
young having fun
Life for me isn't easy.

Chilling with my boys
smoking blunts
telling jokes
talking about God knows...........what
with only thirty bucks
I had to give it up
to be a stronger man and
a better son
enough was enough
awaken everyday
to only play X-box 360
I had to get away
Life for me isn't easy.

All these girls
on my back
calling me a fool
bugging me about
this and that
my moms lecturing me-
about school

telling me to get a job
they don't know
it's hard
Life for me isn't easy.

So I began to pray...

Dear Lord:
show me the way
I am tired of having nothing and
I am tired of being broke
I just want something more
than hope
show me Lord,
show me the ropes
Life for me isn't easy.

I know individually
we must handle our own responsibilities
as men
but, I attempt to try
then fail
it seems like nothing
ever goes so well
my boy died in front of my eyes
alone I still cry
half of my friends are doing bids in jail
I want to write them
but I can't even spell
it's a struggle out here
where I live
some of us don't even grow up
like normal kids
I don't want to end up in the pins
so today I repent
from all my sins......because
Life for me isn't easy

Thanks Thee The Lord

Thank you Jesus
For life down on earth
When I get to heaven
I will thank you first
Your father is a king to me though,
I can't see him
Lord please forgive my repentance
For I am now dependent and
Worthy of his name
I want to make a change
Dying on the cross-
Seemed impossible
You proved it to be true
I want to thank you......again
You're truly a friend!
What you've done is remarkable
The power you have is unstoppable
I want to be an angel
In your throne
Take my soul
Tell the devil........ leave me alone
I don't want demon spirits in me
He is mischievous and devious
His actions is grievous
I don't want to be like that
I have too much love to interact
Why can't we all be the same?
Are Adam and Eve to blame?
In the Garden of Eden
The apple was eaten

Now look at the world today
Corrupted with money and food and land
Clothes and people and places
Properties and races
Goodness gracious
Can we start again?
With a better beginning
To have happier endings
Send your disciple down to earth
Everyday there's a new birth
Is that your way of making it work?
I just want the world to be full of
Joy and happiness
Love and great pleasures
Unity and peace
Harmony and glory
A time that is not poorly
A place where there'll be good grace
No matter what race or space
We would overcome the devils taste
Let us lift our spirits and become one
For our God
We owe him one!

Courage

God you are my friend
When no one else can hear me cry
There are times
That I am locked in my room
Praying to the sky
For things to be better
That's when you give me courage
To try and
Get it together!

Unity

Throughout many years pasted
Some people couldn't make it
Off of the grass
During those times of pain
Others hurt them and strain
What was going on?
How could this happen for so long?
Where was the love and peace?
For those pep's

Many families were broken and torn
Their babies were taken
The moment they were born
All done for benefits
Damn those idiots.

It's hard for us to survive
There's no choice whether we live or die
It's our decision to be righteous or sin
Where there is a lost there is a win
Where there is good there is bad
We function improperly until we realize what we have

Focus; listen to the mind's right conscience
Wrong can lead intentions opposite
We people are raised differently
Realistically we're all the same
Human beings that grow and change

Our cultures and races

Complexion and faces
Diverse languages
Doesn't give us power
We're formed into groups
To unite teamwork then devour
To visualize accomplishments and problems
Faced on earth from birth

See, the world is filled with many materials to profit
These things can cause conflicts
To prosper we need each other
Harmony and unity
From one another
Then spiritually we can concord a piece of this art
God has given us in our hearts

To God We Pray

A dream
we all seem to have
is different
wishing on stars
far away
to God we pray,
above we show him love and
give him thanks-
as we live each day.

He is the only man
that understands
we can change-
so he continues to love
us all
the same!

III.

As I See It

We are all human beings, we grow to know and learn new things. Throughout life we are challenged by things and expected to make decisions that may not always be right. At a certain age we hit that stage where individually we are the caretakers of our own responsibilities.

Leonna Brabham

Poetry

Poetry
A spelling bee
Words to meet
A feeling
A song
A piece of harmony
A beat
Music to my feet
A rhyme in my mind
Analyzed
Repeatedly utilized
Standardized
Consciously mesmerized
Poetry
Mixtures of writing and literature
Languages spoken with knowledge
Spirits holding me hostage
Experiences and lyricist
Embodied in everybody
Formed in a structure
Writing in motions
Feelings and emotions
Visualized in the mind
And written on paper
Poetry

Magic

I am Magic
Like a magician with a rabbit
My life is visible
See me now
Soon I will be invisible
Hidden and away from you
Just watch-
Watch,
What I can do

Then and Now

When I come up
They will try to put me down
That's when I'll tell them
That was then and this is now'

As they continue to talk about my past
How I use to be broke and smoked and stole-
Slept around with guys for cash
There'll call me trash from the past

I would laugh
Smile,
And stand proud
Because I am different now

And yep, I've had my share growing up
From the Bronx, to Harlem, to Queens, and Brooklyn
dump
So go ahead and put me down
Cause that was then and this is now'

We Rise

From the bottom
To the top
We began to crop,
We've made it off the farm
To better ourselves
and bear harm,
I'll tell you' it wasn't easy
But we folks worked hard
and fought strong,
Now look at us today
We continue to rise
From the past of our ancestor's prayers
We no longer stray
In the hands of people
Though it may seem that way
We are mentally lethal
Don't be fooled and confused
The statistic you thought you were
You are not, I'll tell you-
A thing or two we should stop!
Suffering from lack of convention
and start paying attention,
We are not the inferior America has claimed us to be
We are superior, you and me
Let's get on track, don't look back
What they want us to see is…
Pain and poor and misery,
Do not represent an excuse from the past
You show them an example of our future class
Let us lift our heads and stand tall
Our fight between human rights will forever remain a war

Me Time

My food is done
the dishes are washed
the table is set
the house is clean
and the kids are gone
I'm ready to get it on
Finally some me time!

I'm going to wine and dine
with no man on my spine
controlling my every move,
no parents on my back
telling me what to do and how to act,
no sort of contact from my crew
wording in my ear
of gossip and despair,
Finally some me time!

I'm going to walk around the house nude
no one will (dare) intrude
while I am burning scented candles
and watching television scandals
not even a mouse will come out and bother me
I'm going to plop on the couch, (quietly)
then stare in the wall view mirror
making different facial expressions
check out my body and my hair
look around, no one is here
Finally some me time!

Broke in New York City

I'm feeling broke
and down
no money around
all my bills are paid
food is in the kitchen
the lights are switching
the gas is ticking
and I've got hot water,
Still, I sit empty handed
stranded from another world
wishing I could travel the 50 states of America
But I'm broke in New York City
Forever

Tight Like Glue

They say black people can't stick together
Never ever-ever-ever-ever, well,
Whether they're right or wrong
we're strong
Separately
Individually it's shown
that we're smart
No matter if where together
or apart

We came a long, long way
from home
Now that we have arrived
to the throne
They see we are not alone
Therefore we don't have to stick tight
like glue
We reunite as a crew
Yes! We continue to fight
But, everybody does in my eye sight

Black, white whatever races
still faces the basics.
we're not indifferent
you won't dare stare me wrong
us black people got it going on--
no matter what we do as people
Everyone has a struggle
to go through

Anyway we do have some colored people
in the candidacy
Maybe not the majority
but I see--
Don't sleep on us
because when dirt turns
to dust
We'll have much more love
than lust

All I Need is a Pen

Are you ready to write?
Yes I am
How should I begin?
Well, All I Need is a Pen
Then, whatever I imagine
and feel
Will began to shape--
and fall in place
Hey you're right
Just write

The Love of Friends

I love my friends
They love me too
From sin we've been through thin
We share what it was like back then.
Growing up as a kid and teen
We were a team
I love my friends
They bring joy, laughter, and amusement
Like music
to my ears
I need them
when, no one else is-
there, they give me popularity
and care
Like my fan club
always everywhere
We are a crew
I love my friends
They love me too

Materialism

Our main focus is to look presentable
If our demeanor is not just causal
Though some of us have the finer things
We must think beyond dreams…
Nice clothes, nice shoes and nice bags
Means nothing
If you're not worth something
We need assurance in life
To be certain times will be all right

If you're intellectual and social
Let your manner be respectful
When someone approaches you
We never know whose watching
So to get the best profit $
We have to keep cropping
Besides an occupation
We're glamorized by attractions
What's going to be people's reactions?
When you start acting

Our appearance represents our parents
So of course they had to set good standards
Money orientated
Is good when you're family related
And maybe we don't have enough dough $
So it is not who we know
It's what we know
It's all about characteristics
Money just makes the world materialistic
To have the finer things in life is painless
We all would love to be famous!

Rainbow

A sign appeared on the ground
When I looked down
What did it signify?
Of the sky

Standing drenched in the rain
A rainbow came
Beaming art
How did it get there from the start?

Shop Addict

Money, money, money
Then broke again
We spent it on--
Food, clothes, shoes, sneakers, hats, bags
and jewelry
When is the next check coming?

Judge That

Without no job–
No car
and no house keys of my own
You may think I am stressed
I am not,
You may look at me
and see less
But self-motivation is what
I know best

Without money flashing
No new shoes
and no new clothes
You may think I am broke
But I am stashing
See,
I am not lacking those things
I am devoted
To more purposeful springs
I love the most–
Like fulfilling my dreams…
For a good home I can call my own

With no cable
and Internet–
No radio or phone
You may think I am bored
and alone
I am not,
I have scored valuable goods

I can adore-
Like candles
and drinking wine
Meditating in my mind
Enjoying life explicit
Blissful design,
Concentrating on my-
Soul tact
For critics
To Judge That!

Apple on the tree — like me!

First a little seed
Bears on a tree,
Then begins to feed
It self free

Like me!

Turning into an apple
Red, green, or yellow fruit,
Suddenly rotten
From a world that is pollute.

This luscious
Delicious crop,
Once beautiful and scrumptious
Is now on top

Becoming juicy and sweet
To the core,
After you eat
You crave for more.

That apple you love to eat
Is me,
For sure!

Be Alarmed

Friends are good to have
Especially your better half
Sharing lots of laughs
But when things change
Those friends complain
Rather then pertain,
Maybe if people weren't so judgmental
Life would be much simpler
Could it be that we're all biased?
Characterized as potential liars
See how people come and go
We watch and we know
Then assume we're right
When actually who are we to say,
"That's Their Life"
Some say… keep your enemies close
Well, I say…don't
Some say… if you can't beat um
Then join them
Well, I say… nope
We can't continue to hope-
People won't do us harm
I say… Be Alarmed!

Different

We laugh at others
And never stop to ask ourselves
Are we provoked by folks?
When to them we're also a joke,
And looked at differently

That's Life

You may not like me
Or what I wear
Talk about me
I don't care
That's life!

The Hood

In the hood we smoke that chronicle haze
Puff, puff pulls, we visually dazed
Now we head to the liquor store
Plans to get high some more
With the pep's having a ball
Money in the bank,
Pocket change
Eat it up like cake.

Guys on call hitting the cell
Eyes low looking sexy and swell
Scary, wondering, if a move could lead to-
A kiss and tell,
The hood is misunderstood
We're thorough all through the boroughs
Survivors through struggles
And tact's and troubles

We grew up in the projects with roaches and rats
Still, we're better than that
Karma, domestically drama, tame, pain-
Hand cuffed, locked up, locked down, and chained,
Unexplained nonsense
Money on our conscious
That's the number one problem
Yet, we get gangster and solve them

Criminally taking advantage of because we're thugs
And the system was designed for modernity to fail
Designated in the mind of our past--

To be behind first class
Do the math,
We hype with a load sum of cash
Thinking wisely but spending fast

Communities flop whenever there's a drop
It's a war out here
Living in possibilities
Can't declare responsibilities
See the hood is just no good
Giving no opportunities
We will make it though
Because we're just that thorough

Only God Can Judge Me

Some people say… "I am not who I suppose to be",
Well then, who am I suppose to be?
Because only God can Judge me!
I may walk and talk for people to see-
Don't think for a moment that's just me.
Today, I may be calm and sweet and silent-
Tomorrow, I might be loud and mean and violent.
At the end of the day when I pray-
Only God can Judge me!

Success

Does not mean (rich and famous)
It is the power to have gain-
What we've strived so long........for
Meaning, anything in our........ reach
Money is not the major issue
We're living in this abandoned nest
That has us confused,
Breaking up families and homes
Leaving us abused,
Crying for money instead of love and peace
We choose,
There is no limitation to financial rehabilitation--
So why suffer in this nation?
From being broke
When there is hope
Happiness is not always found
Within our wealth
Rather, the achievement in--
Our self
Yes! We are materialistic
Suppose we walked the earth naked
Like animals explicit
Will we be different?
Or there is nothing, that-
Can change our images?
Of greed—
Because there are some things we just need.

The Dream Seeker

We look at the sky and
get different thoughts
The moon and stars and sun
are what we've been taught
When we see those things
We wonder
Who? And how
Then our dreams
are sought
and brought
Into
Existence

Honor Before Glory

When is it going to stop?
The killings and the shootings
Guns pop-pop
Beef and crooked ass cops
Don't help us
Just work
Make problems worst
Too many innocent people
are getting hurt
Dying faster than a bullet
Wonder why the cop had to pull the trigger?
To slaughter another person they thought
was an endangered
NIGGER!
Honor before glory
Not at the ending of that man story

Families get no justification
Only a jacked up explanation-
with no substantiation
Whether right or wrong
The system will prolong
People be alarmed
Murder is a felony charge
Cops possess a badge
to disregard
Honor before glory
Never that…
Never that…

Envious Style

Tired of people
   staring
      intensity
I get a look of
   animosity
      thrown
        at
           me
As I speak
   walking by
      no reply
        they whisper
          behind
             my back
Then laugh,
   did I miss
      the joke
      about
        my ass!!!!!!
What did I do?
   to upset you?
      I get it-
My high maintenance
   appearance
      is
        bad
To top it off
   with
      this
        Louis Vuitton

bag,
You have
   to be
      mad,
My shirt
   My pants
      My hair
         My nails
            ticks you-
I have the
   Beyonce`
      look
         irreplaceable
            you're
               "Bugaboo"
She did say,
   "Diva
      was
         the
            female
               hustler"
So, get
   your money up
      or get
         thrown in
            the dumpster,
You trash-
   no name brand
      wearing
         bags
            clocking
               my stash

I see you
     rolling your
          eyes and
               sucking your
                    teeth
Spreading those
     lies
          to make me
               look
                    cheap,
But you can't
     bring me
          down
I've got
     too much
          going on
               now
Just watch-
     back is arched
          heels are high
               outfit is fly
                    makeup is done
Here I come,
     stunning the
          envious crowd
               with the
                    latest styles
To make ya'll chicks go WOW!

We Are Who We Are

I decided
to write this book
for you
to visualize my point
of view
to me
people are special
and beautiful
Having their own ways
of acting
and reacting
Since the day we met
I've looked at you
as a friend
Although, there were some things
I did not like
I knew, you were just living
your life
At the end of the night
everyone exhales
We are Who we Are
There's no escaping
ourselves

Mission

Visions of the future
Memories of the past
We began to contrast our paths
Are we actually on the same route?
Years and months gone by--
Still at this place
Don't know why?
Cluttered with no space
Steady we try,
To get ahead in this world
Seems like a stream
Everyone is on a mission
To fulfill their dreams!!!!!!

Rain

Drip drop, drip drop,

Rain falls from the top,

Hits the earth for plants to crop

Stop rain stop!

People are looking like wet mops

Precious Child

O' precious little child
Don't cry
Here's a tissue, dry your eyes
Mama will be right back
No need to put up a tantrum like that
You know better
O' precious little child
We welcome you
There are toys, books and plenty of snacks for you
Everything is going to be alright
Don't be scared and frightened by us
We are nice and kind people
This school is cool
We'll have wonderful times.
O' precious little child
Don't fall down
You're not alone
Soon mommy or daddy will come and take you home
This will be fun
Look at the other boys and girls ready to play
They're your friends whenever you stay
There's nothing to fear
In our daycare
O' precious little child
This is only your first day
Tomorrow it will be better o.k.

Hair Beauty

Girls wear those weaves
to enhance those inches
to make everyone believe
those are real extensions,
We black girls don't try to be white
and Puerto Rican
we just like--
our hair to get the best treatment
Curly, wet, or wavy,
box braided or bone straight
It doesn't really matter
If the texture fits our face,
Natural hair color resembling Ebony
Dark and lovely
or yellow like Ivory,
We have top beauticians
that know how to style
In the best conditions
to smoothen our scalp,
Pin it up into a due be wrap
then let it hang down to our back
preserve that beauty
maintain a good rep
It's our duty
to look our best
Get-um girls!

Imagine Me Different

Imagine me a human fish
Walking on two feet
Breathing in oxygen
Sipping Poland Spring
I continue to envision
These imaginary things
Diverging my surroundings
Creating a new earth-
Where we don't have to work
Everything is free and equal
for people
Animals have to pay
Isn't that hilarious in a way?

The Talk of the Streets

They thought it was true
When someone said what they heard
Listening to those folks speak
From another mouth word
Running me down
When I wasn't around
Not knowing what was right
or wrong
Until facts and witnesses
came along-
With proof of accuracy
I don't know why those folks
kept talking about me
See,
All that time spent
Watching me in resentment
Brought mystery to their eyes
Surprise!
It is I on this book
That's right, look
At this star, bright
Aiming far, right
Talk about it
Those who doubted
I don't care
Good or bad
I will still
Be glad!

Playing Your Position

One day I sat on the couch wondering-
How could I encourage people? And help out?
Where can I go to find things I need to know?
In this world we have a position
to follow up on
It's in our mind telling us right from wrong,
We adapt to the universe
Pulling us in-
and pulling us out
Stimulating what we're about
Make yourself visible
Make yourself suitable
Make you known
This world is humongous
You're not alone

The Period

Women are like the moon
When the cycle begins to change
We do the same
Looking to the sun of a man
To brighten our day and land
With our gloominess and presence
We're needed as well
To produce and breed swell!

My Dream

Today I look at those people who decide to fail
and start to notice-
We're one of the races
That does not prevail (easily)
From a history of pain and poverty and torture
Most of us are still suffering because of our cultures
They don't see what I see
Things are a bit different now
We're (free)
Although society tries to keep us down
Where low-income families are found
I look beyond misery--
and stand tall
They can't hurt us anymore

Martin Luther King had a dream that-
"All People Should Be Equal"
Then came white and black sequels
Now, we share fountains and schools and bathrooms
Today I have a dream that we'll be equal
To wealth and health
Incomes and decisions
Thinking wisely and being smart
From the heart
Of our people!

Liberty's Slave

Feel the pain I have embodied
From my ancestors graved bodies
I carry the name of liberty's slave
on my back
Where I keep history,
Because of them I will not lack
Live my life in misery-
For no woman nor man
Why would I be a slave?
Is it in my blood?
But, I am not a thug
I can not be chained and tamed and drained
across this land
By neither woman nor man,
I have too much pride and hope
I cannot be tied to any rope.

In this new modernized era
Let's build our own cultural schools, churches, and
businesses
to keep our people together
Like Jews and Indians and Koreans stick together.
I cannot be working minimum wage for 7 dollars and
change
When I have bills that need to be paid
Slave…. not I
Over the years wondering, why?
We've been shattered and battered and tattered
One by one it was done
To confuse us and abuse us

Don't try it now
No daughter or son of mine shall be simplified
in this new day and time
When our great-grand's were young and small
They suffered and struggled from being poor
We weren't always like that
We are not taught the truth about us blacks
Our race is more powerful than we realize
We lack because we are not familiarized
If they could see us folks now
I wonder would they be proud
and what would they say?
or are we still slaved today
In some hidden way

God's Blissful Place

Where is heaven I would like to know?
Through the clouds what beholds
Past this earth
God's blissful place
Delightful and wonderful
Pleasures of grace
Where the sun beams bright
Through the night
Where cars, trucks, and chaos don't beep
as you sleep
Commotions and dangers that seems rudely disturbed
are not heard
Neither thought of
Happiness and bliss spreads out love
Through this place above
Sinful tension is stopped at the gate
To prevent scattering hate,
Where is heaven I would like to know?
For that is the one place I dream to go
To another land
Where the great man stands

Imagine Me Skinny

If I was slim
Imagine who I would be
With a model star banging body
Just imagine me skinny and this pretty, Wow!
Guys would be tripping, drooling, dreaming and
fantasizing about me
Though they do it now
Just imagine how it would be to see me skinny,
Wearing a bikini thong
Dancing in the video for one a Jay-Z songs
How flattering would that be?
To see me-
Sporting a tube top, mini skirt and a pair of fresh Nike's
Posing for King and Vibe magazines
Flexing the boom-ma-ness body ever seen
Picture me with a fitted dress
Big ass and Big breast
Walking across the room entertaining guest
Well, I guess you would love to see that
Instead of me fat
Hum-hum,

The way I stray down these streets
I don't need to be skinny
I represent Big girls trendy
My shape is sexy
Never once was I called messy
My style is top notch
Skinny I am not
I don't dress to impress

or use my body as a fling
I don't sway like I'm some-thing
I'm always on the quest
Coming on the set
Looking my best
and it's just naturally fresh
For folks to see
I laugh at all the fat jokes
Only, because there funny
When some girls just want to be me
So, just imagine if I was skinny
and this pretty
Hum-hum!!!!!!!!

At The Club

She stood there sipping Champagne
Dancing to that T-Pain song
You watched
Her hips move side to side
Waiting to catch her eye,
The club, it was packed
In fact at capacity,
The music was jumping
One girl had you bugging,
Loving her style
Pretty smile!
Sexy shape
and gorgeous face
She was worth your while!
As she continued to dance seductively
You never stop watching
She was worth every dime in your pocket
One drink would be lame
Her appeal was a bottle of champagne
and the change,
There was something about her texture
That called for a sudden lecture

Approaching her smile
Through the crowd
Catching her stare
In the air
Before long, you went over there
To greet her presence
Of pleasantness

When you began to speak
You blurted and joked,
She was sweet and nearly choked
It brought a spark to your spine
A hint to your mind
She was so god damn fine!
Such a kind
Taking your hand
She began to wine in front of you
To be continued…
At the club

My Sister's Couch

We all slept there
At your place
On your couch
You did not say a word
Nor did you ask for a dime
You let us in with open arms
All of us,
From family to friends
When times were rough
You were so nice and giving
During those times of living
We ate well and stayed fresh
Never did you complain
We were there too much,
Together we laughed, talked and cried,
On your couch
No one was ever kicked out
Sincerely because, we respected your house
Even your daughter shared our love
When we laid on the rug
Cuddled in blankets
Watching movies
Drinking martinis were our favorite,
Everyone brought joy
To your house
On your couch!

Peaceful Tree

Beside this peaceful tree
I sit quietly,
On a bench with my pen and pad
Picturing,
All the imaginary things I wish I had
Daydreaming intentionally
To design inventively
As I see,
The tree of nature
With fallen leaves and broken branches
Still, I've chosen this spot to sit in silence
Along with whistling birds
and sneaky raccoons
Gathering my thoughts of life
I began to see the light,
Looking up into the sky
I talk with God
Feeling my spirit react
I can tell a response came back
Turning to the tree
My mind sets free
Meditating as I think
Suddenly, it hits me
Life needs more at peace
Like this tree

Current Events

Who-is the person?
What- is the matter?
When- was the time?
Where-was the place?
Why-is the reason?
And how-is manner?

My perspective of this lesson in class was to craft
Like Art and Math
We learned to draft
A skill we feel can prevail is worth doing
Brewing yourself can help
Meaning:
Before we make that sudden move
We're given the opportunity to choose
As we flow through current-
Destined is predetermined
We don't know realities next move
In actuality we assume
It's our own character
That operates like an adapter
A plan given before hand is a map
Graphical representations to lap
Perhaps, the outcome differentials
There will be issues, see-
Current events is presence
Who:
What:
When:
Where:
Why:
And how is the message

Reality Show

Cut on the TV
What do you see?
A reality show or video

Designed to side track
Our minds, lost of time
Since color televisions came about

Too much negative foul mouth
Easily influenced by the attraction
From people singing, rapping and acting

Wonder why our kids live life for fashion
Even the white kids are slacking
Glamorized by televised actions

What happens if we don't have the talent?
Are we left to feel less of a person?
Forced to make our lives worsen

Everybody's reality is not a show
We need to let our kids know
How to get where they want to go?

Young & Dumb

(She Smiles)

"Young and dumb" is what they called her
When she would stay out late
and cut school
Smoking all day, sexing older men
To her was cool
Then she got pregnant and people called her a "fool"
Because she needed welfare for food
Baby daddy left her cold and blue--
Now what is she going to do?

Well, I'll tell you...
She is going to be all good
Finding her way out the hood-
Watch how she grow to know-
The mistakes she chose
Her kid matters the most
Forget those hoes
Calling her "young and dumb"
She had to learn on her own
and have a little fun
Now her time has come-
To work and quit welfare
While her kid is in daycare
Success is almost there
As she looks ahead it is near--
Reading books with knowledge
She rides the train to college, **proud**
Planning a better life for her child
Because running the wild life is down
She smiles!

The Matter

A day of peace
Away from the streets
Of negativity

A day of happiness
Smiling, laughing and bringing joy
With righteousness

A day of pleasant experience
To everyone's appearance
And parents

A day of no violence
Arguing over nonsense
And guilty conscious

A day we can share
With care and love
And hugs

A day commodity doesn't scatter
And no longer are we battered
Matters, To Me

On Our Own

We left home
and never looked back
We were alone
and young at that
Living on our own
We couldn't relax
We learned from ourselves
How and where to seek
This made us stronger
When we were uneducated and weak
From house to house
We slept on couch after couch
Living out of bags and buckets-
suitcase luggage
No one cared
and no one wondered
This is why we just left
and continued to try and
Do our best!
On our own

The House Once A Home

The rain
was the hurricane
that came
crashing down
the house
mom and dad built
Long ago-
we watched
from a near by window
doing nothing but watch
from a near by window

Little Girls Want To Be Like Me

Singing on stage
with my stunner shades
Gliding my legs
Grinding my hips
I am a pro at this
Little girls want to be like me
I'm an actress
and they see attractiveness
Pretty on TV
Staring in the movies
Receiving all the designer material gifts
to keep me crisp,
Little girls want to be like me
I'm legit
Why? I ask
Is it the cash?
Or the attention I get
I bet that's it,
Attracted to the glamorous life
and I'm famous right,
Little girls want to be like me
Studying my act
Daydreaming she could do that
Practicing my moves
Singing my tunes
Watching me on DVD's
Constantly playing my CD's,
I seen her at my concert screaming-
Jumping up and down
I couldn't believe it she was me all around
Little girls want to be like me
And when I was their age I also dreamed
To be like me!

Judged Different

I lived in the ghetto
I know the streets
Hello!
Most people there been no where-
But I'll tell you…
Them some smart people,
Though they are wild
Known to be loud-
Society has framed them to be like that
Mainly because their Black,
Outsiders don't care if they kill each other or not
As long as they don't chill on them folk's blocks,
To them, we're nothing but, low budget-
Mc Donald's Mc nuggets
Crown chicken meals and dollar deals-
Chinese food rice and bargain price
Welfare and childcare-
Section A will pay,
Gang bangers and thugs
Selling drugs,
Music and rap
Guns and setback,
Thieves and hoes
Crack heads selling clothes
Roaches and rats
Glued mousetraps,
Babies and young ladies
Sex after sex
Color should not make us less,
It is not who we are-

It is what we've done
and that's how we'll be judged
When that day comes
So continue to look at us differently
and hate our swagger
Your opinions will never matter
To me!

IV.

Dedicated To Family And Friends

(Featuring poems "About the Author")

Family is an ancestral bond. Generation after generation we enlarge. We must stick together as a unit and be there to care with love and support. Before you know it someone has deceased off the earth and it is too late to make peace. Then all that is left will be the shared memories. Hold on to your family!

Leonna Brabham

I Am Love

Hello!
They call me love and mellow-
with a sweet and pleasant attitude
to show for gratitude,
I am a person revealing righteousness
Through feelings, experiences and consciousness,
Watch me closely
Read this well-
You will see the character I prevail…
Every aspect that I define
Is heavenly divine
I have my bad days and ways
God said' "whoever prays stays"
My faith is in his judgment
So I repent.
More about me--
I am smart
I am content,
I am morally hearted
and a hard worker once I get started
Strong and open-minded to the books of knowledge
Helpful and supportive
Encouraging people positively
Because negativity will not bring prosperity along--
Continuously…doing wrong,
I am a great debater
Portraying the ambitious mind of a negotiator
I am wise
Through these poems you will see my strives
I am persistent

A surviving inner spirit,
I am a woman with style and grace
Someone you could love and embrace
I am a beautiful woman with class
Never forgetting the route of my ancestors path
I am the future and hope of this generation rage
Visualize my poetic thoughts to make a greater change
We all can be free from emotional past
And be all we can be at last!

I am me, Self- Explanatory!

American Black Poet

Because, I believe in   accomplishment
I am confident   of what I do   and to me dreams
                    come true
            So I wrote this book for you!
                    All the people
                    All the faces
                and all generations
                Here is my creation
Have this gift   I give to the
                    world
        The talent I had since I was a little girl
                This is my legacy
                For you to have and see,
            Enjoy every piece of this art
Written in the language   from my
                    heart
            Don't take my work as hurt-
                It is simply the truth
                Of what we do-
            and how we act as people,
I'll take it back   if you feel it
                is whack
            Please forgive me for that.
        And let us not allow our troubles to
                break us down
        These poems are here to lift your spirits
            When I am not around-
                My visions are explicit
                Expressed like magic
Practice   after   practice
                I thought of you
                Watching me
                Eventually,

                    I began to see-
Who I was as a person   and this was
                    it...
          An American Black Poet!

My Purpose

To follow my fate
and seek strength from within-
My positive conscience mind and
I shall survive,
Believing in me will determine my wealth,
Exceeding my worth by working hard and saving first
My purpose,
Is in me, with support from friends and family
And God, he is power and shower
The purpose of my life every second and hour-
He is light shining on me
To see, my destiny
My purpose,
To show kids and peers and elders
I am a great leader because they are the reader's
My purpose,
To use proper language and stop cursing-
Because insolent people are no role models for today and
tomorrow
My purpose,
To judge no one by their appearance and actions
To indulge in that is the "Law of Attraction"
My purpose,
To pursue anything my soul desire searching
As I practice and study to be perfect!

Determination

Would you like to make a difference?
Like other people that have in the world
I know I could
Because I am a bright girl
But, with no money to invest
How could I build my nest?
I want success
Potentially built I will turn outstanding
Straighten up from a tilt
Imagine me on the billboard standing--
With a stunning stare for publicity to declare
I know that girl she did not give up
Determined to get through-
I have to make it for you.
I want to be like me
So all the people could see, what I see--
On a positive note
Because of all the chronicles I wrote...
Proud of myself,
All it took was:
Patience
Practice
Persistence
Potential and a lot of help--
Then, determination
Strong-mindedness
Certainty
Confidence
Convincing
Intelligence
Proficiency
and talent
Eagerness to pursue
With my capability I resolute

Grown Up!

I am self-
Explanatory
Territory, notice my style
Is not wild
When I enter a room
In my head
Ahead, right to left
My best
At the people I left
Staring
By attraction
My beauty
I don't have to present
Structure
My mother
I am fully-
You can't take
Me
To even try
Men won't do
Wrong
Too much
Automatically
Exceptional
Special
Show my
When I've got
Mature
Protective
Own set
I am
Well

when you enter my
my character
all about me!
music plays
I began to bloom
I put forward
glancing back
gleaming
glamorized
not only by
but, my actions
my curves of
the resemblance of
is shown
grown now, and
advantage of
I'm too.........sweet
to beat
me harm and
I've got
woman going on-
they see I am
and treat me
there's no need to
ass!!!!
class, it pays to be
and self-
to have my
prospective
grown-up and
respected!

Why I call myself Lovious?

I'm true to the colors

I discovered a mathematical configuration

Considering that we met

I'm taking that into consideration

I can't jeopardize your life

It's your decision whether you want to be wrong or right

I still have to live for me externally....

When you're gone, literally I'm left alone

Physically and mentally planning a life of my own

Existence is created difficult

I'm not that simple

I decided if I show some love

I will resemble,

The L in my name gives me the obligation to proclaim
Lovious

You can only blame yourself for your own actions

They've your attractions-

That's why self-explanatory I'm officially love

If you know me you're liable to get a hug

More than likely, I'll speak to you first

Even if I'm mad it won't hurt

Being the bigger person always seem to work

Thuggish, roughest, toughest bully is Lovious!

Angel Eyes

I see the best looking girl when I appear in the mirror
My appearance represents my demeanor
Regardless, what people think?
To me I am all!!!!!!!!!!!!!!!!! That
and can't be told otherwise,
In my eyes I am a prize
Walking and talking with style, I am proud
I am love sent from above.
High self-esteem describes my every meaning
I fit on every team-
By applying myself to the fullest extreme,
Pleased with my precious gestures
I speak and give people lectures,
Those who hear me know I'm special
My smile lift spirits
From feeling down to terrific!
I am not a selfish person
You won't catch me screaming and cursing.
I communicate instead of acting unkindly
My texture is so divine
I feel great pleasure in my heart
If there's trouble I don't want to be apart,
I dance and sing around my house
Nothing scares me not even a mouse.
I am jubilant and free
I am beautiful and thankful
I can hear and see
I can feel and smell
I can taste,
I am happy to be alive
Heaven waits for me to arrive-
I am an Angel in their Eyes!

Seek Out

I'm a girl with so many dreams
Possibilities taken to the extreme...
With plans for the future and hopes for tomorrow-
Which way should I go?
Tired of procrastinating and moving too slow-   -   -

How can I achieve what I want in life?
When nothing seems to ever go so right
It may sound crazy
But I admit to being lazy
At times I loose control and become unfocused
and everything around me becomes unnoticed

Here comes the down fall
Back at square one
Hanging out, partying, drinking and getting high just to
have fun
Are my proprieties straight? No
Am I setting good standards for myself? No
Can I change my habits? Yes
Then try to get things established? Yes

Don't just say "I am"
You can do it, I know you can
Strong and built for the job you are
Get out there, don't make things hard
Times may seem difficult to handle
Have faith and courage in yourself
Then take others help

You are smart
Yet you want to be apart of nothing
I understand your actions girl
But how long are you going to take in this small world?

The time is now
Take care of your business now
You know how,
Worry about you first
Then others later
They'll still be there do them the favor
Don't slow your pace
For something that is a waste
Because you will loose your space

Your destiny and mission is possible
Seek your reward and don't let anyone stop you!

What Do I Want To Prosper?

Finally, I asked myself that question
Tired of hopes and assumptions
So, for now on I'm making adjustments
I will add more everyday
To achieve my goal, I'll go all the way
Studying what I've learned
To make something earned
I want to be a professional writer
So, where do I go to establish desire?
I would love for the world to know my name
So, how do I find fame?
I am confident others will enjoy my work
So, I continue to write like I'm already an expert
One day I will be familiarized
By those already stabilized
In this field
And they will also say "she is skilled"
Surprise! Take a look
It is "I" on that cover book
Yes! It is "I" on that front magazine
I am now living out my dream
What do I want to prosper?
How about......... I succeed!

God Is Amazing

O! Thank God for this book of mine
I've been truly blessed
With such unique rhymes
Writing night and day
Some how got complicated
So I began to pray...
Asking the Lord for strength and wisdom
To do my best
Without the stress
In response I became focus and gained knowledge
Using words and metaphors
I never knew existed
Even in college I was convinced-
I had skills
and often told
My poetry felt real
At times I was impressed
My work was actually
Flattering
When I expressed,
Feeling rhythm in my soul
I danced alone,
Praising
Giving Thanks To God
He Is Amazing!

Singing, No Blacks Allowed

I dedicate this to you-
I can relate to some things you go through
Life can be challenging, I know
With a world that is crucial and favoritism and difficult-
Scarcity,
See, this society is bullshit if nobody is here for me.
I am stranded in a community;
Watching those who succeed don't look or give back-
In deed we're in need
Greed, envy and desire and grasping, is what we're facing.
The world is drastically changing
We as youth should start behaving and participating, more-
Stand by your native land
Hand and Hand
Potentially, there's a possibility we'll make a difference
We're the new generation
We've come too far to stop now
Look at us, wild, beastie and ghetto
Is that what people want the minority to believe?
Well, I know better
See, my folks prayed and my folks stayed
Succeeded and got paid$$$$$$
So why disappoint them now and go back to being slaved-
Black to the back of the bus
Black to the back of the line
No blacks allowed, no blacks allowed
Yelling and screaming loud
No blacks allowed singing no blacks allowed.
Old folks can't and won't go back to being broke, picking
cotton

Down South history will never be forgotten
and Hitler for the Jews I'm sorry for your departed
I know the lost was broken hearted.
This world is one big nest-
What a whole… lot of mess
Protest, prolong, procrastinate, do your best!
Don't forget this earth was built to work functionally
Not to hurt eternally…………

From Me to You

I give my all
Nothing less than I am
Nothing more than I could afford
Here,
Share my love
My time
and my joy
A greater wealth to enjoy

Encouragement

In front of hundreds of people I stand firm
Excited to give a speech
Deliberating what I've learned.
In this industry of poetry
I've written words of knowledge
To make us wiser
and stronger
Be aware-
Seek what is out there
In your eyes-
Concentrate on what you're destined to be
You shall succeed
Do not be discourage by those who don't commune
I encourage you!

Family Tree

We are a family
We are a whole
Don't you know?
That's greater than gold
The love and support
We share as a bunch
Means so much to us

A dynasty is important
It means everything worth supporting
The touch never goes away-
Never goes away…
Though some days are different
and difficult
We shall not let our weaknesses
Get to us,
We represent a symbol
of togetherness
Our unconditional fondness
Shall forever be an abundance
To share

To My Brothers and Sister

Dear brothers and sister
I am you and you are me
When we're not together I think about you all the time
You never knew
But what I do, is especially for you
It is hard to watch you grow knowing we're all different
Still, our looks do show.

Life seems shorter if one of you is not involved
That's why I must address any problems unresolved
We are blood, through genes no matter what
and I love you all so very much.
We're true family and partners
Siblings and friends
Since we were little kids
Our joys and laughs have been real
I feel--

Nothing makes me happier and proud
Than having my brothers and sister around,
Every moment we share shall never shed
We are a bond with many memories spread
No matter what happens in life
Remember every word I ever said…
My purpose was to brighten your day
and put a smile on your face!

We are like a cookie; each of us holds a bite
My piece will never be eaten, Psych!
We are like pie; each kind Nana and Grandma ever baked
We represent the whole of a sliced cake
We each have our own dreams, hopes and routes to take
Good luck brothers and sister on the choices you make!

A Daughter's Dedication

(For my Mother)

MOM; MY SHEPERD

I Love you so much
Queen of my throne
Dignitaries of the life you've shown
are noble
In my eyes you deserve a prize
To embody my spirit
Exemplify your character
Through cries and laughter's
You are emotionless
Though pain cannot hide

MOM; STRONG ENOUGH TO SURVIVE

Why stop your life for mine?
Me being the middle child in the mixture
With three brothers and one sister
To see us develop birth to maturity
Blossom into the earth maternity and paternity
Fascinations of your five kids
Reactions to take, actions to give
and daddy did he ever make you happy?
Honestly, do you consider your life bewailed?
Satisfyingly fulfilled

MOM; REALIZE I'M NOTHING WITHOUT YOU

Continue doing your best and never feel any less of a
woman
Picture this:
A big house, backyard, a great job, nice car, expensive bags,
shoes, and clothes…
The luxury life an American dream holds
Does that sound anointing to your grace?
Beautiful and flawless surrounding your face
Beneficially you deserve the world
With me as your designated baby girl!

MOM; DON'T CRY

Dry your eyes, in do time I will provide
What you want and need because I love you so much
Wait! Did I thank you yet? Please! Don't let me forget
Thank you and thank you again
For being a wonderful mother and friend!

Daddy's Little Girl

(For my Father)

Dad you've been in my life since day one
To watch me grow--
Why did you leave? I don't know
My entire childhood you were there
To share
To care
and take me everywhere--
Things changed
When you left the house
It just wasn't the same
Without hearing your mouth,
I wish you could've stayed
Days would have been better
But no, it was wetter
With tears of thoughtful years
Memories of us as a family
You, mommy, my siblings and me
All happy!!!!!
Daddy's little girl I was
Receiving kisses and hugs…
Laughing and playing-
Feeling the love!
We share a resemblance you and I
Same hair
Same nose
Same eyes
Same lips
I am;

Your rib and your hip
Though at times I am sad
I'm happy you're my dad
See,
I learned from you to strive--
and to always try,
No matter what…Never, ever give up!
You always told me "I'll soon reach the real world"
Well, I never understood as a young girl
Now, I am fully aware
Life is not all about fashion wear
I have bills to pay and business to attend
Meals to cook and clothes to wash
So, thanks to you I know what and not to buy$$$$$
You'll always be the #1 man in my life
Along with God and Jesus Christ
Like an apple on the tree
You protected me
Until my time came to adapt to the earth
I was set free--
Experiencing love and hurt
To find what I was worth$$$$$
Dad,
Aren't you glad? Aren't you proud?
Of what I've become
Thanks to you a job well done!

Sister

My sister means the world to me
I will do everything to protect her
We're connected forever--
Like semi twins
No matter what
We'll be together forever
She is my best friend
and I promise to love her past the end--

I love you Ebony C. Brabham

Brother

My brothers are my shield
and armor
Helps me through karma
If something bad ever happens
It's going to be drama
My actions will show
and they already know
I will never let them go--

I love you Leon, Arnold, Andre and Allen

Bright Star!

(To my niece Jaydah)

Hey bright star!
I see you beaming far
While sleeping in bed
I watch you dreaming ahead--
Even when you're not around
Glow is found

You have many hobbies--
You love toys and books, games and parties
Your favorite is Barbie's.
You adore singing and dancing and watching TV
and you love to write just like me!
You love fame everyone knows your name
You're sweet just like the candy you love to eat!

The smile upon your face is beauty!
Like art designs you shine
Little princess you're a gift to us-
We love you so very much.
There's no need to worry
When you have our touch,
You're an idol
With your talent you'll be a good role model!

As you grow, I want you to know--
I'll be here
Don't fear troubles
Think of life as a bike
When you didn't know how to ride you cried
Then you did well after you tried
You loved it!
The key is don't quit
And always remember good practice makes perfect!

My Recognition To You

(For my Nana Stephanie)

Dear: Nana
I want you to know that you're great
You are a woman of grace
Thanks for the moments to remember
Thanks for the memories we treasure
A place in my heart
A place you'll always be apart of,
Your love is magnificent
It keeps my pain away-
Because of you I learned to pray
There's nothing I can say,
There's nothing I can do
To fool you

Your birth was a woman's worth
You raised my mother to raise me
In return this is how I turned out to be-

A mixture of you both
I thank you for the poems I wrote
The talent you have
Has passed on to my soul
Now it's my goal
To get accomplished,
Because of you I am confident!
You're a righteous individual
Your personality strengthens me to be wise-
About any decision-making

Throughout the many obstacles and risk taking-
One of mine is losing you
I only dream about tomorrow but,
I cherish today
Anything is possible
That's why you educated me to pray.

I am a gift to you
Produced by a woman
Delivered by you
I want to give you more assurance in life
To know you'll always be all right
So, here is my appreciation
and anointing truth
My recognition to you!

Grandma's Intuition

(For my Grandmother Helen)

Always on the go--
Full of activities for me to know,
You give me insight on life
As I continue to grow--
You've made your skills visible
Your talent does show.
I learned from you
To be a woman of independence
and how to get by on my own--
Because some guys are full of stupidity and ignorance;
I'm better off alone.
You're a cultural woman
Strong on our roots
You have inherited African and ancestral traits
This makes you intelligent and wise
In other people lives,
You're able to give me useful knowledge
to create
A circle of hope!

When we talk-
I listen to your words of wisdom
We address every issue
You often encourage me...........optimistically-
You've inspired me in many ways
I expect to retire like you one of these days.
When you come around
A gift of seriousness

Is always shared
I know my siblings and I are important to you
and you only want us to be prepared-
For a world full of responsibility
So you constantly express your love-
Through morality,
You're always on the go--
I already know
If I am going your way I must be on time
Or I'll be left behind.
From you, I found the values of art
and Grandma, your intuition and support
Will always remain in my heart!

My Mother the Queen

Mother:
First person I seen when I entered the world
Nine months inside her womb. Out comes a baby girl!

Mother:
Love her
Shower her
Hug her
Kiss her
Embrace her
and respect her

Mother:
Look into her eyes, because of her you've arrived, genetics
cannot lie
Why does her face look just like mine?

Mother:
Makes you laugh when good times are thought of, her love
will always be around when- you're down; she is your other
half, no other person compares to the way she is there.

Mother:
To let you know
I'll never let you go
First on my list
With God's heavenly bliss

I want to say I love you in a special way
Each and every day
So, I Love you and I Love you more......

For Nana-Banana

Banana-Nana, we shall never split
Whatever tomorrow holds
I'm with you from up and in.
Though days seem shorter
Our love is stronger.
Memories of laughter-
From jokes and character,
Here from day one
To share and care with fun
Teaching us God and Jesus Christ
The way to live life,
You're grand and mother
Like no other

Happy that you're truly mine
Through spine-
You appear more than often
Showing concerns and offerings
Giving our family more than a gift
You are devoted
Something priceless
Its togetherness-
Keeping us warm and comfortable
Your presence is always enjoyable,
What are they going to do without you and I?
From up and in--
To the sky!

Best Friend

(For Saudi)

Over the years we've grown-
and became known
To each other's way of life
Sharing a history
of good times and bad
Now we can look back on the past
and laugh,
Those memories
Bury us close
with hugs and tears-
When we struggle and hope.
From cool to tough
We never give up!
We get along now
Better than ever
Treasuring every secret
Forever!
Don't ever feel I love you any less
How could I?
When you're the only friend I call Best!

Heaven Sent

For Jaydah my niece & Myasia my goddaughter

God bless these angels

(Jaydah and Myasia)

Two bright girls

Always in my world

Blossoming into the earth--

Chosen since birth

To make me happier and stronger

No matter what goes wrong;

They'll give me a reason to continue on--

Thank God for you children heavenly bliss

A sensational feeling I will always miss.

Two angels in my eyes

I will always have them by my side

Love you dearly

Love you both

Here to help and there to coach

Hoping they trust and understand

That I am their right hand

When I am no longer around

Look up in the sky where I'll be found-

Or, you can find me in your heart

There, we shall never be apart!

Baskin Robbins

To my girls
All!!!!!!!!!!!!!!!! 31 flavors
Long lasting life savors
Ya'll know me
We're a variety
Different banging bodies
Occupations and hobbies
We are a mixture
Posing for the picture
Real women, divas and queens
Along with assorted dreams--
On the scene
To make the guys fiend
They say'
"It's hard to choose like ice cream"
And men, would love to taste all
So like the store
They come back for more--
Some spices are off limits
And they just can't hit it
Opp's I meant get it (Ha-ha)
Still, we vary
There's plenty options
We are popping!
Like Baskin Robbins
One lick-
Can kick
The original chick
To the carve
After you've been served!

A Special Dedication

This one is dedicated to you know who
My poem, my song, my book, my award
That's my word you're my trophy and prize
Realize you've brought victory to my eyes.

I would say "yes" at anytime to be your wife
You've brought fortunate luck to my life
Happiness is shown all over my face
In your presence and at your place,

We've done so much together over the years
You've been there for me with open ears
And time will only show
I never want to let you go--

I want to share everything with you
Not just partial
You're my rib I can't live without you
We're the greatest couple!

Love, I dedicate this one to you
Exceptionally and extraordinary remarkable
I believe we belong together
To build and be pleased forever--

I've chosen you to be mine
Today, tomorrow and due time
Share my love, my world, and my life
My greatest gift to be your wife!

You know who you are
Soon to be a star
I want to build with you
Have your kids and marry you
Ask me
I'll say "I DO"
And make you the happiest man
Living on this land!!!!

The Creation Of Jaihsir Crawford

From the man to the woman
A new creation was delivered
A baby boy named Jaihsir
Is now here
On earth you are
Rising like a star!
We'll watch you grow--
and get to know
How handsome and intelligent
You'll become
In my eyes you're a prize
God will watch over you in disguise
Continue to pray with your parents
To suit a better appearance
Laughing, playing, working and praying
Is the route you should be taken
A phenomenal and sensational look
To see a family grow so well
Like being at church together before12
and having in time while everyone else is outside
You'll learn to see/hear/smell/taste and touch
On your own
and one day leave home--
I want you to remember
"A GOAL IS WHAT YOU WANT"
You'll be a man one day
and if you continue to pray
You'll be o.k.
Every year you shall turn a greater age
and hit another stage
This is a blessing for you to stay on the right page
Love You Jaihsir!

She Is Proud

(For Nancy)

Does she really want this baby? Yes, no or maybe
She sets in her room contemplating,
Alone, with her stomach developing a child
Feeling proud!

Yet, unsure what she would soon have to face
She closes her eyes and visions began to take place.
Rubbing the spots that hurt
Wanting everything to work

Crying to sleep
Only to dream her life to be complete,
Cranky and painful in bed
Twisting and turning from thoughts in her head.

Carrying pregnancy symptoms
Gave her signs of wisdom
Because women are like the moon
As the cycle appears to gloom!

Five more months to go was all she needed to know
Then five months past and a baby boy began to grow-
Looking like his father and mother creation
Taken the name after his father relation

To nature she brought Amin Lewis
Hoping her decision was right
She has chosen to just live her life
Without the fright-

Insanity did not deprive this family
Loving and caring
and times of sharing
When their hard work and dedication became over bearing-

Doting every moment of motherhood
She is thankful to have understood
How nurturing her child felt so good
and she'll do it again if she could.

Enjoying times of craft
Watching her son laugh,
Still taking care of responsibility
To be sure her son could eat.

Stressed when times got rough
She considers being optimistic will make her tough,
Establishing a different route
Since the baby came about-

Associating with friends did not stop totally
Moody and emotionally
Still, she loved the company-
Especially with her son, she is never lonely.

Putting up with other people ignorance
Put more pressure on her conscious
As she and the dad stables one another
She remains focus on being a good mother.

Managing her personal life
Sleep does not come much at night,
But with her son by her side, she cuddles
and snuggles all the time,

Loving the physical closeness of her child
She is forever proud!

I Guess That's Why. . .

I remember when I was just a tot
My mom held me a lot
Holding me into her arms
Loving her kids like lucky charms
I guess that's why today we shower her palms.

She would say, "Baby when you all were born everything changed"
Even with two before me things just wasn't the same
There were still more kids to name
I guess that's why after me two more came.

As you could see I am the middle child
And because of that I will make my mother proud
Show her I could be like Queen Elizabeth and where a crown
I guess that's why I try so hard not to let her down.

I didn't like to see my mom upset and sad
So, at those times I tried to make her glad
I'll help around the house and keep things neat
I guess that's why today I am well organized when we meet.

I love the way her texture feels when she hugs me
So comfortable and cozy
I miss her when she can't be found
I began to frown
I guess that's why today she is always around.

Now it is her turn to watch me prepare for success
And be proud to say' she led me through the right process
When I look at her I see a mother of five beautiful children-
Helping and rebuilding
I guess that's why today we express our feelings.

I am so enthusiastic that she brought me into this world
To be such a bright girl
And stood by my side from good times to bad
I guess that's why she is the best mother we could've ever
had!

In Memory Of Fly Tye Written In 2003

Dedicated to: Floyd Quinones family & friends
(October 4, 1974-- April 30, 2003)

In the mist of the dark they claim he was reaching for a
ratchet
So a cop shot him in the back without even asking
Now look what done happen a rookie not even a captain
Tried to get paid by taking another life out the P.J's
They even gave him years in the pins
Lord, I know he wasn't perfect but everybody sins.

Came back on the block and still made it to the top
I knew him as Tye; I was never around for Floyd
And the pigs went and took away that boy
I wasn't around to see him be brought up in the world
But right before he deceased he left me the name "Fatty
Girl"

He lived a happy life behind he leaves three kids and a wife
It hurts when you lose a friend; it never really hits you until
the end
I'm crying as I write wishing he were here
Every time I walk on Carlton Avenue. I miss him being
there
Thank you for being Tye; a very nice guy
With a chip tooth now in the sky
Why?
This man was celebrating his dude birthday
Like a soldier and you took him away

Tye was our friend and our brother he was a son to his
mother
They haven't won fun just begun
War in the Fort not Iraq better call the president, we about
to attack

Now, I'm upset because I watched him lay in the casket
It won't be the same without him
We'll miss his smile
Wow!
In the mid-morning he laid fruitless on the ground
Soon he was taken away
I couldn't even say "good-bye"
So, I asked God why? Why couldn't he stay?
Was it really his time to go? Could we ever know?
His girl just had a baby boy named Amir
And now his daddy won't even be here to watch him grow

Much love to his family and friends who miss him to
He was one of Fort Greene finest doing it for years
Still, he watches over us crying in tears
Let's toast with a bottle of Hennessey he didn't just drink
anything
We will miss you La Pa-Pa best known as Fly Tye
You're gone now but always remembered in our hearts
No one will ever break that apart

He Lay

In Memory of Wille Roy Kenner
05/15/1968--- 08/22/2007

Be not afraid to cry, for a love one just died
Bereaved sorrow, can't go away tomorrow
Don't wipe the tears away, we shall all weep someday
Exhaustion will be drained, from salty water and human
rain
Pouring from the eyes down onto the face
Conceptualizing an image never to be escaped
All to remember, a once known member forever--
Manifesting in sadness, beholding the madness
"Roy" was characteristically happy and enthusiastically
smart
A sensational feeling everlasting in the heart!
You shall overcome, this troublesome, some day--
Seek a touch of love, and a friendly hug
From a mother he was:
Your son, your father, an uncle
Look again, that's your man and your friend
Worldly departed, leaves you broken hearted
Together we sob, as times get hard
Find a shoulder to lean, a place to redeem
Here is a tissue to blow
I know, I know, I know
You're hurt; someone you love has deceased off the earth
That's painful; whoever is to blame should be ashamed,
Last moments spoke with bliss, will be missed
On a tense night, through the dimmest light
You'll feel his silence
Don't be afraid to cry
When you glimpse the sky

Stars will glisten as someone up there listens
His presence is now with God we pray
As his flesh is put to rest
He lay

Rason Jones Forever Known

(*July 28th, 1982- November 1, 2006*)

From us to you
Family and friends
Whoever he knew
Celebrate a special holiday
[The creation of Rason Jones]
Forever known

Deceased off the earth 2006, November 1
Still loved and missed in absence
We breathe his presence,
How could he exist? Then perish

Life is not meant to an extent
Let's turn from sin and repent
Keep love in our hearts
So when we depart we won't be forgot

Memories of the past, mostly good times we had
When days were happy and sometimes sad
I dedicate this poem to you
A friend I once knew

Recognize you're missed
I wonder can he actually see this-
When I think of him and picture his face
Sadness, unhappiness, and tears appear

I want to escape that feeling
But I can't stop the thoughts of us chilling
Hurt and broken-hearted
Torn from his departed--

He gives me strength to smile
Can it be possible that his spirit is still around?
Personally I wish this message be retrieved
What's the real reason he had to leave? Causes of dieing
could be anything

In the beginning of time Paradise was first designed
Then men and women began to decline
Forgot about their roots
And became accustomed to the fruits

Now we live in prosperity and negativity
I don't know what after life consist of
But here he's truly missed and loved
Bless his soul and spirit
Wherever it goes--
Everyone knows he was terrific!

R.I.P Friend. . .I'll Find Your Spirit Again

In Memory of Rason Jones
(July 28, 1982- November 1, 2006)

I walked up the block one day
Didn't see you there
Fashionable clothes you would wear
Fitted hats to match with expensive kicks
Pockets stacked with bricks of cash
You kept a cup in your hand
and walked with a dash
Flirting with all the ladies as they strolled pass
R.I.P Ray
We'll miss you everyday
It's so hard to say good-bye to yesterday
I sit in memorialize times we shared
of a good friend that cared
Awkward feelings since you disappeared
Sent to a better place
Even though you were hood
Heaven shined upon your face
Because when you laughed it revealed much grace.
I knew you for years we were like peers
Back in school
Hanging out was cool
I'll never forget how charming you were
Though you had a temper
You were always known to leave stupidity alone,
As we get older we began to think wisely

People are not born to last so they die surprisingly
On any day during anytime
Gone before you can say good-bye
Family and friends gather for the memorial
To get one last look before the burial
Hurting and crying out in tears
From all the thoughtful years
Seeing you go was unfair,
Bless your soul wherever it goes--
Spiritually, I could feel you live still
Don't know where but one day I will
This is not the end
I'll always remember you dear friend!

For My Friend Tiffany

In Loving Memory of her mother Miriam Wilson
08/01/1951-- 12/08/2008

This nightmare I live
Will never go away
I am awake
The thought of you gone
Can't be escaped
I miss your face

It was painful for my siblings and I
When it was time to say "good-bye"
We were weak and
Broken
Sick to the stomach
and choking

Still, no distance
Keeps us apart
Your existence
Remains in our hearts

When I cry-
My insides hurt
At night the torture is worst
My heart burns
When I want you back
You were my mom
No one can ever replace that

People say they can feel my pain
But you were my best friend
My life has changed,
A part of me remains empty
Still with all the sympathy

You were beautiful
I am happy to take after you
and share your smile!
People who knew you
Look at me now
and see I am your child

What shall I tell my kids when their born?
Now that my father and mother are gone-
I'll show them a collection of pictures saved
Then reminisce the good old days
When my parents were around
Feeling their spirits shining down
and miss them the same as I do now

Forever Torn

In Memory of Harmeek Allah Shamblee
01/18/1991- 09/19/2007

September 19, 2007 another young boy died in violence
Shot and killed in Fort Greene Projects,
I need a moment of silence...
Back from a thoughtful conscious
I am Torn,
When is this nonsense going to stop!
These communities are not safe for us to crop
We don't need to be living here
Fighting with our peers
Hearing the news that a friend just died
Makes you want to cry
and not bring your kids outside
But why hide?

Sad and upsetting
Heart broken and depressing
No one deserves that lesson,
Death is granted
From day one it was planted
Does that give the right to take someone's life away? No
We can go a different route
Instead of killing each other
Think about working things out
Become friends instead of enemies
Better off associates than loneliest
Commonsense

Don't you know we already exist in a dangerous society?
Prosperity for self-
The more time you spend worrying about someone else
Disregards your own wealth and priorities

That's one reason why people can't handle their own responsibilities.
So-
I wish things could be different
But, my decision alone isn't enough power
We must ring as a choir
Picture his once born face, erased
Remember his presence that took place
Do it for his love and grace
Make a choice to love or hate
I'm sorry a friend of mine died today
and it hurts inside everyday
To think of little "Meeky" gone
I am Forever Torn

Remember Me

When I am gone
Far from long
Think of me as you see-
In your mind, in your soul and in your heart
We have not depart
But, in the world I don't exist
For now I am truly missed-
As you play and sing and dance and laugh and cry
in sorrow
Memories will follow
Still, I will not be there tomorrow-
Remember me
Bright, nice and polite
Always talking to be right
The typical type
Everyone liked
Open-minded to the mic,
Remember me
Sweet and pretty
Like a melody song
Living on and on…
A tune so deep and strong,
Remember the words I ever said…
Poems I ever read…
Moments we ever shared
Remember when I was there
Suddenly a tear,
It's obvious I am no longer here
No matter where I've gone-
Remember that day I was born

5/15/84 as you live on…
I maybe watching from another place
with honor or disgrace,
Stay on the right path-
Equivalent to God's craft
Save yourself from the (curse)
Before you vanish off the earth-
If you forget me
I'll no longer be around
Love doesn't fade away-
So remember me………… as that day……….. we were
together
and I'll be in your hearts
Forever and Ever!

A Job Well Done!

Many people have inspired me
Someone is reading this
Someone is listening
and someone is watching
While others are waiting for me to arrive
Here I am giving thanks to all
Those encouraging me to be wise and strong
To continue on…. no matter how long.…..

Thoughts and opinions of me has taught me everything
Actions and attractions has influenced me repeatedly
I've improved,
I am now more confident
I am now a role model for the future generation
Because of you I am patient
I am happy my life is no longer complicated

Thanks for the inspiring words
and all the criticism I've heard
You all deserve the recognition
Because of you I turned out terrific!
You've lifted my spirit and made me cry
I now realize the glory in your eyes

You all cared and shared hopes of me becoming successful
I stand before you to show my appreciation
You all are my dedication
I'm addressing all of you
Thanks for making this possible!

A shoulder to lean
A pot to stream
I now believe I can achieve anything
Inspirationally you're my strive
Again because of you I'll continue to try...

I survived having nothing to become worth something
I'll never forget the people who guided me here
It feels so much better to hear you cheer
I am pleased and satisfied with the outcome-
A job well done!

Coming Soon My Next Book Of Poems...

It's pleasurable and full of sparks!

Including *He's the Player* and *She's the Player*

He's The Player

At first he was around
and did things to make me smile
then he just left
Leaving me stressed
with our child-
Why would he do something so foul?
Without talking it out
or leaving a note
Taking something serious
for a joke,
How could he not care?
About being there...
Day after day he wouldn't call
I was at home doing it all
Playing both roles of a parent
Setting good standards,
I refused to be sleazy
So I did it well
to make my job easy
Preparing our kid for school
and being stressed over this fool
Was not cool,
At nights I cried and tried to move on
Just when I found myself getting strong
This deadbeat comes along
Trying to play dad
Thinking I'm suppose to be glad
After struggling too long
with the little I had-
He honestly thought his bags of stuff

Meant enough
When he's been looking fly and buffed
Polished up
Sleeping with several women
Like I didn't know
When he got someone pregnant
on the low-
They prank my phone
When he left them alone
to gossip
Feeding me with their whole concept
of what was going on
Bugging me while I'm trying to move on
I couldn't take no more
But every time I'm doing better than before
He comes back knocking at my door
and just like any other time
I play blind
Letting him in raw
Because of the past, I continue to adore
and the future, I continue to ignore,
I wonder if our baby was better off aborted
Tired of being with a guy-
That doesn't find us important
Cheating with excuses that are useless
I can't keep trying to give my kid a father-
Who is ruthless
It's just not fair
To be with a man who is never there
and doesn't show that he care

She's The Player

This time it wasn't him
Who cheated and lied
It was I,
Why?
I don't know
As we continued rapping
on the low
It just happened
Things got out of hand
Soon I forgot I even had a man
and wanted to do me, see
This other guy made me feel different
When I talked he really listened,
I loved his style and his smile
He was a clown
with ever joke I giggled
and every touch tickled,
We went to places of a dream
and he always told me nice things,
Whenever I tried to leave
He pulled a gift out his sleeve
and then told me to chill
So he could express how he feels
My babe for prior years started to complain
About how I've changed,
My phone was off
I was never home
So of course he suspected
I wasn't alone,
We had an unconditional love

Since high school I was his drug,
He treated me right
Some things I didn't like
Although he called me his wife
This other guy seem more my type,
I admit
I went too far
with all the messages, massages, dinners and gifts
I accepted
We started sexing
and it was good
I wouldn't let that go even if I could
After being spotted in his car
I should've stopped
But I liked him a lot
My man just couldn't let me go
So I played him on the low
Eventually, things got out of control
and I was called a slut, bitch and hoe
Smacked and pushed and shoved
All because I played
With love!

Shout Outs

To all the people that brought this book and actually read it, thanks a lot. I hope you all will enjoy my poetry the same way I did writing it. To let you know it only takes time and self-determination to make things possible. Everything else will follow. Never give up trying and don't ever feel discouraged. Your talent means nothing if it is wasted.

Dear: Maya Angelou I am enchanted by your poetry. One of my dreams in life is to meet you; maybe one day you could read a poem of mine, feedback is all I ask from a poet who is gifted. Your voice is beautiful, and your poems are magnificent. In everyway you inspire me. You are my "S-hero". To Oprah Winfrey, you said "What material success does is provide you with the ability to concentrate on other things that really matter. And that is being able to make a difference, not only in your own life, but in other people's lives". I want you to know that with this quote alone you have made a big difference in my way of thinking. I want to do more, to give more and feel good about it. You are phenomenal! I look at you as an idol. To Barack Obama our First Black President! You also inspire me. I knew you would win. You are brilliant, encouraging, and your actions have also changed many people lives. Good luck in the White House. I have faith in you. YES WE CAN!!!!!

Shout out to Full Vision Records. I see you "Blake" on the come up. Shout out to Soketah's hair beauticians and barbers in Brooklyn, on Myrtle Avenue. I hope you all like the book! Anyone who wants to look their best, I recommend their perfection. Special shout out to my best friend Saudi you're always there no matter what and you always have my back. Over the years I've learned to talk with you more and I see your strive. I love you girl! I know I called you constantly for your help, what can I say' you've been smart ever since we met in Junior High school when I copied your homework. (Ha-ha). Well, I am done. My book is finally going to manifest. I hope you're proud of my biggest accomplishment yet and Good Luck to your success! Shout out to Fort Greene projects for showing me love. Special shout out to Walt Whitman side, named after an American poet. Unquestionably, there is talent in Fort Greene. God has introduced us all for a reason. Shout out to my friend Nancy for always listening and loving my poems. I also appreciate how you've lend a hand with this book and never once did you deny me your time. You were more interesting in this book coming out than I was. You are also smart, thank you for your support. Tiffany M. your view influenced me to enjoy the process of writing this book. You have the face and talent of a star, thank you! And I will be in Pennsylvania with you promoting it; you know how we do, (Holla!!!!!) Tiffany W. thank you for caring and hyping me up, you are multitalented and proficient at what you do. My heart goes out to the lost of your mother. I hope you like the poem I dedicated to her. To Ebony H. you're a strong woman. Taurus!!!! I see a lot of potential in you, just believe and stay self-motivated as goodness appears within your life. Thanks for wanting to hear my poems and the input on the titles. Love you Myasia! My beautiful Goddaughter (heaven sent).

Now, Temekia L. we've been good friends since elementary school and for some reason we're always on the same path sharing different occupations. God is Great! We will forever be friends and keep singing. Your voice is lovely. Thank you for being a true friend. Nasiyr even though we just met in college I see your passion for poetry. You keep it real. Thank you for your advice. Good Luck to you. To my cousins out in Jersey I am shouting you all out for always coming around and showing love. We always share the most laughs and I see ya'll doing it BIG! out there so don't forget to pass the book around. I love ya'll so much. Big Rahmel thank you for giving me props and cooking all that good food, I don't eat pork no more but I will never forget the times when you called me "Pork chop". (Ha-ha). To my friends, all 31 flavors.....and others, sorry I can't name everyone because it's too many of ya'll and I don't have that kind of money yet, for all the pages, (lol.) but you know who you are; we watched each other grow from childhood representing Fort Greene Development, I don't know why we call our Communities "Projects" but anyway, we're grown up now, most of us have kids (not me [yet!]). Ya'll know I still love the kids; I give you all the utmost respect for being good mothers! On the real, we're all living our lives and moving away from the hood but no matter what we always get back. So, this book is to our friendship; whether I am there or not for the comments, thank you for mentioning it, I love you all! Now if I forgot to shout you out, my back, maybe you just didn't notice my talent but please still buy the book and maybe you'll then see my ability to strive. To those who waited on the outcome of this book your support means a lot to me! Tell a friend to cop their own copy.

At this time I would like to give sympathy to all my friends who lost members of their family. I know their remembrance can leave you feeling alone. They're gone but never forgotten. I hope my poems enlighten you and I hope you'll cherish the one I wrote specifically for you from my heart. May they forever Rest in Peace. God Bless!

About the Author

Leonna Brabham resides in Brooklyn, New York and does not go anywhere without a pen. Her unique style is expressive on paper. She is currently a Journalist major at Kingsborough Community College, with plans of furthering her education to achieve a Masters Degree. During childhood years she wrote and recited poems with her sister. The passion was always there. She then decided to present her own art of poetry to family and friends. She went on reciting at schools, churches, clubs and special events with every opportunity presented. Her audience wanted more and that's when she became enthusiastic about writing "All I Need Is A Pen." And like magic her work continues to appear on paper.

Leonna brings to you her first collection of published poems relating to every aspect in life…that may also relate to you!